heroes among us
Uncommon Minnesotans

heroes among us
Uncommon Minnesotans

Jim klobuchar

Pfeifer-Hamilton
Duluth, Minnesota

Pfeifer-Hamilton Publishers
210 West Michigan
Duluth MN 55802-1908 218-727-0500

Heroes Among Us: Uncommon Minnesotans

Printed in the United States of America
10   9   8   7   6   5   4   3   2   1

Editorial Director: Susan Gustafson
Graphic Design: Jeff Brownell

Cover photos clockwise from upper left: Charlie Brown, Linda Phillips, Dorothy Molter, and Jimmy Bowman.

Photo on page 112 courtesy of the Carl Isaacson family. All other photos courtesy of the Minneapolis *Star Tribune*. Most of the material for the article on Amy Klobuchar appeared originally in *MPLS–ST. PAUL Magazine*, whose publishers have graciously granted permission to reprint it. Several of the pieces are original for this book and the remainder appeared originally as columns by Jim Klobuchar in the *Minneapolis Star* and the *Star Tribune*.

Library of Congress Cataloging in Publication Data
95-79014

ISBN 1-57025-085-5

This book is for Abigail,
born in 1995 into a world where
there is still room for heroes.

contents

introduction

Uncommon people flavor our lives. One of the most appealing people I've met as a newspaper columnist was a boy in the mountains of Nepal, a kid to whom I've never spoken. We made contact by waving to each other across the thunder of a Himalayan river. I'll never forget his face, and never lose the yearning to meet this boy again. We seemed to be gripped by some mutual hunger to know and understand each other. That meeting appears in this book, along with others that put us in touch with lives that seem in different ways to give color to the day.

Except for the super celebrities who flash by on the carousel of our TV sets—the entertainers, athletes, and talking heads— we don't often stop to define what makes some of these people extraordinary.

The celebrities, although they may be attractive, are not usually the most memorable people in our lives. Who do we remember best, apart from those we love and befriend?

We remember the men and women (and sometimes the children) who shaped our lives, directed our minds and impulses, sometimes without knowing it. We remember the piano teacher with the wild hair who managed in some disorderly and frantic way to head us down the road of loving music, which became a priceless gift. We remember the earnest screwball in the neighborhood who was always inventing things and never amounted to any cash success, but we remember him both joyfully and tearfully because we have never in the rest of our lives seen a person try so hard.

We might remember the nonconforming athlete whose kinky refusal to look or sound heroic put some balance back into a game that threatened to become our obsession, or a failed politician in whom we find dignity because of his or her pursuit of an unpopular principle.

We remember the graceful acceptance by a man growing old

and dying in a wheelchair, unable to speak, his life of achievement over, but nodding his head and smiling his thanks to his visitor for taking time for him. We remember a kid, mentally retarded, walking so zealously in a walk to raise money for other retarded kids that he fell exhausted in the middle of the street.

And, of course, there are some superstars that also occupy a place in our personal pantheon of memorable characters.

What appears in this collection is one newspaper columnist's album of such characters and personalities, over a span of thirty years, drawn from his previously published columns. If I had to categorize them broadly, I'd say they are the ones who made me laugh harder or lit my fuses of wonder or anger or stirred my respect. Or they are ones who made me cry in the face of their private bravery or sacrifice while in pain, grief, or triumph.

In most of these people, including the famous ones, there's a kind of X gene, something that sets them apart. That may happen with an idea they ignite or the performance they produce or the presence they create. It's something that strikes us now and unequivocally. It's a quality that might arouse us or shake us up or leave us envious, but there isn't much question about their uniqueness.

The more I think about people such as these, almost all of whom I came to admire, the better I feel about the humanity that makes up this helter-skelter time in our lives, one in which the wandering columnist found himself a sort of recording witness. There's something in these people to draw from. There's something there that elevates. Maybe what I've felt is the comfort of understanding the human spirit a little deeper in its struggling, its unguarded moments, its nuttiness, and nobility.

Do these people have anything tangible in common? Maybe not, except some may be a little more venturesome in their search for what they're seeking, a little more creative or reckless in fulfilling their lives, or maybe more receptive to the quiet grace of a good day done.

Most newspaper columnists, whether they work in the city

or in a cornfield, are the minstrels of the reader's day. Some days they have a story to tell, other days sparks to spew. Some days they perform for their audience; other days they are the audience's voice or its irritant. Most of the best stories they have to tell are the ones of the heroes and rogues who season the day's news.

In here, I hope you will find somebody you've met before, whatever the place, whatever the name.

Jim Klobuchar
1995

the world touches minnesota

Himalayan boy

He was a boy whose name I've never learned. He had lively brown eyes and black hair that flopped in his eyes as he bounded down the mountain path in Nepal. We didn't speak. But we entered each other's lives in a precious way I will always cherish.

Somewhere the linguists produced a word they call "serendipity." It means having a gift for accidentally finding something, usually good. It's a lovely idea, although it's clad in one of the ungainliest words I know.

Most of us assume we have that gift, in the same way most of us feel a streak of extrasensory perception now and them. Maybe we do have serendipity, although it's possible the Scriptures have better words for it. We usually feel cleaner and healthier when we return from a weekend in the woods. We have restored ourselves, rediscovered something calmer and more wholesome than the speed and tumult of the bruising life we lead in the passing lanes.

I don't know whether it's serendipity that comes into my life when I visit the Himalayas in Nepal, one of the poorest lands on earth. I do feel a reconciliation there. I admit being an incorrigible about going to those special hills. I hear a music I hear nowhere else, and enjoy a simplicity, a freedom to breathe deeply, and a solidarity with those who live there.

It may have been serendipity that brought me into the life of a little boy on the mountain path. I do know it was a moment, even though a small one, that I will carry to my last days.

Despite the legends, you probably won't find the meaning of life if you go to the Himalayas. If it were there, Shearson-Lehman would put it on a credit card and set up franchises. But there is so much congestion in all our lives—the need to meet commitments, achieve goals, stay with the flow, charge around at seventy miles an hour—that it obscures our most profound needs. It muddies the importance of our relationships, with one another, with the earth, and with God. It lessens our energy for finding and offering the best that is in us, for giving the service that is within reach of all of us. And it often throttles our education as human beings.

That kind of pace does more. It stifles the harmonies in our lives. And sometimes those harmonies are easier to feel and nurture in a place like the Himalayas, walking through a forest of rhododendrons, looking at summits of everlasting snow. That is the second tabernacle in my life, the open air of nature. Others have their own.

In another part of Nepal, the plains, people live in hard poverty. Life is better for the Sherpas, the hill people. But except for the mountain guides, most of these people, too, live primitively and starkly by our measurements. They grow potatoes at 11,000 feet in little fields rescued from the granite.

One day late in the afternoon at our campsite along the Dudh Khosi River, I went for a walk. The river comes cascading down from a great mountain called Cho Oyu. Beside the river is a huge boulder, flat on top but forty feet high. There was still some of the streaming sun to enjoy, so I climbed to the top of the boulder and sat down to listen to the river and feel the sun.

And there I met a new friend, who educated me and made me feel closer to what God is doing on our earth today quite apart from those great convulsive events that we dissect so earnestly to define God's will.

He was about five years old, his hair topsy-turvy, his face and eyes the color of mountain coffee. He was walking hand in hand with his father behind his mother, who carried a sack of potatoes while her husband carried the tools. They were returning from their small field at the end of the workday and were about to cross a wooden bridge on their way home. They lived in the village of Phortse, 400 feet above the river. The boy looked around and saw me on the boulder. He seemed startled, because he wasn't expecting to find somebody up there. He fell behind his father and waved. I waved. And then he stood quietly as though he'd forgotten something. He placed his hands together, as we would in prayer, his fingertips touching just below his eyes. His lips moved. I couldn't possibly hear him above the white water. But I knew what he was saying.

Namaste. Nah-mah-stay'.

In Nepal it means "I salute the god who dwells within you."

We have language that is comparable, but not much that is more graceful in its expression of goodwill and yearning for a personal peace. Whenever I hear it, I think I have found a better world that day, simply knowing there is such a word.

The boy waved again and ran after his father and mother. At the end of each switchback in the trail up the slope to his village, he would stand and wave, and I waved back. It was not quite a contest. But you almost had to sense that all this thrashing and waving was going to decide, one way or other, who had the longest hangtime. The boy was almost a quarter mile away when they got to the top of the slope. But I could see him through the rhododendrons. And finally his mother went to his side, hugged him as though to say, "This was a good adventure. You have met a friend." And then she, too, waved. A minute later they disappeared into the village.

I would have loved to run up the slope and embrace them and thank them for bringing me into the boy's world. Here was an aging and comfortably well-off American and a poor kid from Nepal. Our needs were so far apart, but we shared the need for discovery and for acceptance. One planet, yet so many different worlds. And still we are much closer to each other than we realize, in our frailties and our longings. Of all the ways in which we try to make some sense and recognition of the other worlds besides our own, this may be the best.

Here was a memory: A boy closing his eyes, touching his fingertips, and praying to that spark of divinity in a stranger, a spark that he shared.

It was something to carry away, and to keep.

those who serve

Linda phillips

Some of Linda's ashes will fall on a lady's slipper in the woods near Seagull Lake a few days from now. That is not a prediction. It is practically a decree, pronounced by Linda.

It will be honored. There are no options. Heaven save the misguided lout who crossed Linda Phillips when she made up her mind.

It will also be honored because no one deserved more than Linda Phillips to lie among the wildflowers and pine boughs that thrash in the wind in the canoe country of northern Minnesota.

The lady's slipper of the north's short summer is a kind of wild orchid, lovely and fragile and intricate, but oddly tough. It is also Linda. The present tense is preferred. Linda was fifty. Most of her life was pain and busted visions and scrabbling years of coping in a wheelchair, that and her undefeatability. It was the kind of life not bound by markers of time or even death.

She was the human spirit pounded by blows of grotesque unfairness and savagery. But like a wildflower growing out of scorched earth, she was somehow adaptable to them and even forgiving of them. She was a gorgeous bride with long black hair and a limitless future. She had brains and guts and looks and ambition. She could have reigned over society galas or stood in a protest line and stared down polluters. She could have run for Congress or kicked the butt of a seal hunter. She was that strong and that motivated.

And then their car plunged over a cliff on their honeymoon in Mexico twenty-nine years ago, and the world became a horror.

It did for a time. All right, the world was never quite fair for Linda after her paralysis. Why should this woman of so much energy and wit and with so many dragons to fight have to be hobbled with dependency? Why was it Linda who would never have children and never experience a day without pain or a day without some lingering symptoms of the might-have-beens?

Why should somebody who heard music in the woods and in the middle of a storm, go deaf? She did ask those questions. Eventually, she came to terms. Others, she said, had it worse. She still had choices. She couldn't run a marathon, but she didn't have to give up being Linda Phillips. If she were still going to be Linda Phillips and stay sane, she had to resist the poison of resentment and martyrdom. Being cantankerous all the time was deadly. Being cantankerous part of the time, when she had a cause to fight, could be productive.

She was never quite sure whether she could make a difference. I know she did and how she did and why the falling ashes of Linda Phillips should mean a little something to all of us next weekend.

They were divorced several years after the accident. There were no excessively hard feelings. Their lives had changed. Each of them carried a separate kind of grief and altered goals. Hers were to revere the earth and living things and to keep her mind restless and honed.

Her immobility first stung her. If you want the truth, it enraged her. God, what are you doing? Then she decided on a wily strategy. She would outwit and outlast her paralysis.

When the airlines refused to let her ride in a wheelchair (that was stone ages ago), she campaigned against them with speeches and ridicule. When that failed, she tried mischievous poems and charm, and she was as good at that as she was with her harpoons.

So she flew. When they said it would be hard for her to ride in a canoe, she found somebody, Wilderness Inquiry, to say it could be done. "We can't go through our ritual of dunking you as a beginner," they said. "Dunk me," she said. They did. She spluttered to the surface, laughing. Wasn't this the most glorious day of her life? she asked.

It was, until she slept under the northern lights and saw a bear and heard the hail on her tent roof in a thunderstorm. Then that became the most glorious day. Storms thrilled her. The electricity in them seemed to restore her inert muscles and charge her emotions, and she would regret it when the storm died.

We met eight or nine times. She became the sister I didn't have. We exchanged secrets. She enlisted me as a conspirator. She wanted to know how she could help save this or that. She needed public assistance to live in her apartment in a Cedar-Riverside high-rise. She had no money, which didn't mean she couldn't make donations. She found two dollars to give to Save the Whales. She gave three dollars a year for retarded kids, usually with a poem. She tried to save trees and rhinos, and if there had been a fund to save anteaters, she would have given to that. If it breathed or if it streaked sap, it was kin for Linda. She wrote and read, and once in a while she would stare at the ceiling from her bed and say, when nobody heard, "Am I really making it?"

I don't think she knew how much she made it. At her funeral services, scores of folks gave testimony. They wept and giggled. They loved her values and respected how she refused to withdraw. They found her wrath hilarious. Someone said this: "Imagine a person having shrunk to eighty pounds, and dealing daily with pain, being so lyrical to imagine herself in the middle of a flower, feeling its colors change?"

Linda never stopped exploring. She made a demand on me one day. "Tell me what you feel in the Himalayas." I said I feel what's expressed when the Nepalese greet each other and they say "Namaste."

"Show me how it is pronounced on this pad," she said. "Nah-mah-stay'," I wrote. It means what? It means "I salute the god who dwells within you."

With her hand, she asked me to come closer. She wasn't crying, but her eyes looked mixed. "Do you believe that?" she asked. Believe what? That something immortal and good lives in us? I said I do. She smiled. I think it was in agreement. And I think she knew more than I did.

She died in December with the request that her ashes should be cast into the woods and water in springtime. What Linda will bring to the northern woods next weekend doesn't have to meet the theologian's definition of immortality. She said she would like her ashes thrown among the waters and the wind of the Boundary Waters, where she once met a lady's slipper. That's romantic and good. But what Linda left that is more important is the strength of her struggle and her refusal to give up her humanity. It makes a wildflower something special.

Jason gaes

In the midst of his first book, the author had a question about his material. The author was eight; his material was cancer.

Do you have to know how to spell it, he asked his mother, to write a book about it?

She studied the rising energy in his eyes, and then his tape recorder and his writing pad. She remembered a June day in Iowa two years before, how he lay in his uncle's van on their way from Spencer to the Mayo Clinic, when the tumor in his stomach was growing larger by the hour, and they talked about living and dying.

Remembering that, she didn't think it was necessary for Jason Gaes of Worthington, Minnesota, to know how to spell all the words in order to write his book.

"My cansur started when I was 6 yrs. old and I was at my Gramma Gaes' house," he wrote. *"My uncle Terry looked in my mouth with a flashlight and saw a bump by one of my teeth . . . "*

By the definitions of the trade, Jason's composition may not be a book technically. It doesn't have much heft. It can be read in four or five minutes. It lacks a publishing house and a table of contents and evidence of professional proofreading. You can't find footnotes under the cartoons drawn by his twin brother, Timmy, and his older brother, Adam, ten.

But the technicians may not have walked into a shower after a radiation treatment, and left it bald, hair washing down the drain. As eight-year-olds, they may not have gone to classes with books in one hand and a barf can in the other, queasy from treatments but anxious to learn.

This is the way Jason Gaes has attended some of his classes at St. Mary's parochial school in Worthington.

It's a book, all right. It's a book because it has a beginning and end and truth as an eight-year-old boy remembers it. It's a book because it understands where it's going and why it was written and who should read it. It's a book because it is the witness of one who has struggled and never yielded belief, but who also has observed. It's a testament, but also a manual. The title by Jason Gaes leaves no room for suspense.

"My book for kids with cansur."

He writes to them about his fright, and theirs. He writes about a treatment he calls "radiashun" and the trap of lowering their goals and discarding their dreams because they had cancer.

He has had it, but his prognosis is good. His chemotherapy treatments have stopped, and the doctors believe that if a year goes by without recurrence, he is looking at every prospect of a full and normal life.

Above all, it is a book because it has a dedication at the end, to Margaret Picha, a nun in Bird Island, Minnesota, the sister of his second-grade teacher last year. She, too, developed cancer. Learning of it, he wrote to her, and they began corresponding as brother and sister. And he has converted her. His counsel: She should live the kind of life she has wanted to live, "because if you are afraid to or don't want to do that, it's like death, anyhow."

Jason's treatment began in June 1984 at 4 A.M., the day after he arrived at the Mayo Clinic in Uncle Terry's van. The family had been bound for Worlds of Fun on a vacation from their home in Worthington to Kansas City, Missouri. In the party were the parents, Craig, a thirty-three-year-old packing plant supervisor in Worthington; his wife, Geralyn (Sissy); Jason; his identical twin, Timmy; Adam; and their three-year-old sister, Melissa.

The worlds of fun began in Storm Lake, Iowa, where the father's family lives and where Jason and his uncle launched into a rollicking game of flashlight, staring into the usual crannies. Mouth, ears, the rest. It was then when his uncle noticed the growth near Jason's teeth. His parents thought it might be an abscess. A dentist examined it and suggested an oral surgeon. Something was wrong in there. The next stop was Spencer, where two specialists performed surgery.

"They came out and said it was lymphoma," the mother said. "The word didn't register on Craig. It didn't register on me, either. Craig asked if it was all right to take Jason home. The doctors just looked at each other. They mentioned the word 'malignancy.' I almost stopped breathing. We called the Mayo Clinic within the hour and drove at night. I was devastated. It was like riding down a mountain, knowing what was waiting at the bottom but unable to stop. I tried to tell Jason what cancer was. He wanted to know if it was like the movie he had seen on television.

"Are they going to take off my leg?"

The mother tried to talk without revealing panic. Cancer was like a cold in some ways, she said. Sometimes colds get worse and become pneumonia. Sometimes cancer gets bad, and people die. She said they were going to see the best doctors there are, and she was sure they could help him.

The doctors called it Burkitt's Lymphoma, an uncommon form of cancer that has a suspected tie-in with viral infection. It often is characterized by the simultaneous eruption of several tumors in various parts of the body and usually is fatal unless detected quickly, before the tumors affect vital organs.

Geralyn Gaes remembers the progression.

The stomach tumor was the size of a golf ball in Iowa.

A couple of hours later in Rochester it had grown to grapefruit size.

Shortly before the therapy began it was ten inches in diameter.

There was a tumor near the optic nerve, one in the mouth, another near the stomach and kidneys.

The therapy evidently disintegrated all of them. The boy lost his hair and regrew it. He returned to his classes as a celebrity. But he is a popular kid, quiet although mischievous, and his ordeal had given him a maturity in dealing with both the misfortunes and the triumphs of his friends. Nearly a year ago, his mother read to him from a book written by another boy who had suffered from cancer. The final page was written anonymously, because the boy had died before he finished.

Jason Gaes reacted angrily. He wanted to know why "kids always die" in books like that. He told his mother he could write a book. It should tell kids what they should expect to face, when they will be scared and when they shouldn't be, but that they should understand their strength. She thought such a book would be beautiful. He ran to his room and began taping his memories. These he transcribed, and started writing. Somebody wanted to know how much help he received.

"The writing is his," his mother said. "The ideas are his, and so are the misspellings. We gave him guidance, but the work is his. He wanted some illustrations, but he's no artist, and his brothers did that. He wrote it on folded typing paper, and he worked and reworked it for seven or eight months. We thought it was a wonderful thing for him to do, and when we had the big party we had all promised ourselves in June, two years after that day in Storm Lake, we made copies of it and used them for invitations. More than three hundred people came. Jason wore a tuxedo because everybody wanted that day to be the celebration it deserved to be. The American Cancer Society is going to publish the book, there's been some press about it and Jason is now beginning to see that his message is being heard."

The $25,000 they realized from the sale of their home in Storm Lake when they moved to Worthington is gone, but the family is receiving some state assistance now. The stress of seeing his twin brother facing death produced an emotional and physical reaction on Timmy.

It induced stuttering, which has not disappeared. But Jason's ordeal and his willingness to transform it into a testimony has radiated throughout his neighborhood, his school, and the community.

"He's just a good, bright kid with faith who has brought a lot of people together," said Sister Margaret, a St. Mary's teacher. He's also a very normal kid with his floppy blond hair and his ambitions to become a football player. He reported Friday night for the first practice of his YMCA football team, which his father coaches. But ultimately he wants to be a doctor, a cancer specialist for children.

"I want to show them that they can have cancer and not die."

He already has begun his work.

In the aftermath of Jason's marvelous book came a film documentary of his struggle, a movie that won an Academy Award. He began lecturing cross-country, and still does. But today he is approaching his eighteenth birthday, cancer-free, a high school student in Marshalltown, Iowa, where his family lives, a six-footer with a girl friend, a basketball player, and a golfer. He has been in remission for some ten years, and all of the markers are good to fabulous.

Myrtle hanson

The patient impulsively began speaking Latin, reciting expertly from Virgil's "Aeneid." Not long before that, she greeted a visitor in Norwegian. When English finally was restored to her hospice room, the place sounded pretty humdrum.

But no one could possibly describe the patient that way, an eighty-five-year-old woman who now is ready to acknowledge and accept—without trauma or dramatics—that her life is ending.

The doctors decided years ago that one of Myrtle Hanson's incidental roles in life was to keep doctors humble. It was nothing she intended, although she did achieve unusual success at it, and she did it with total serenity.

The doctors broke the news to Myrtle back in 1986. Her surgery for colon cancer had revealed malignancy in the lymph nodes, and she had only six to nine months to live.

They spoke to her with that blend of professional tenderness and dignity with which the sensitized doctors of our day confront the doomed.

"Oh, my, we'll see," Myrtle Hanson said when they finished.

There was nothing defiant or ferocious in that response. Myrtle simply disagreed. They suggested chemotherapy as a respectable last gesture. She chose what she thought was a better therapy.

She got reinvolved with her world. She spoke to church groups and she raised money and she even bought a white Toyota to drive some of her friends from church to their homes. She got the car a few years ago, at about the time that doctors examined her heart and found a condition so grave that they had to recycle the bad news for Myrtle. She might be gone any day.

As a matter of fact, she was gone when her minister son, Mark Hanson, arrived to visit her. He found her room empty.

Feverishly, he looked for a doctor or nurse for the explanation he dreaded. What he found was his mother, across the hall, pushing her IV stand and splitting her flowers with a guy who had no flowers.

But just one moment. What is the eighty-five-year-old widow of a Lutheran evangelist, the mother of a Lutheran minister, doing reciting Latin from her hospice bed in St. Paul?

The answer to that gives us a glimpse into the waning life of a pretty extraordinary woman. But it also gives us a wistful look at the might-have-beens of thousands like her—women born into a time less generous to women than the gifts they brought to it.

She didn't rail then. She doesn't now, about being boxed into a Woman's Role. It would have shredded the town elders if she did back then. Imagine the wife of an itinerant preacher picketing the local bank for not hiring female vice presidents in South Dakota in the 1930s.

If she came out of college today as she did when she was 21, graduating from Augustana in Sioux Falls, South Dakota, she could walk into a dozen industries that need somebody bright and verbal and ethical to fill a job. They're no longer bashful about recruiting women. To tell the truth, they're rather eager to tell the world that they're doing it.

She graduated magna cum laude and won debating championships. She taught, and she met and married a man whom she loved but whose work her own life simply had to revolve around. He was a circuit preacher who was so busy that she practically became a single parent. It was the style. It was the culture, and it was practically etched in the stained-glass windows of the church. It was the world sixty years ago. Today she could have married the same man, had her children, and made it in politics or banking or law, if that's where her energies moved her. She might also be wearing a white collar herself, which means she might have been a preacher-politician and either gotten elected to Congress or invented another synod.

She recited Virgil the other day because a female attendant at St. Joseph's Hospital in St. Paul wanted to pray for her in Latin. Myrtle remembered her own from college. They got together. The only thing missing in that scene was the two of them alternating between "A Mighty Fortress" and Gregorian chants.

I know Myrtle Hanson just barely, a white-haired woman, strong, quick, and alert, one of those people you feel wired to immediately. I know her well enough to hug her in church and to tap into her vitality and to grieve now that her cancer has spread to the point where the doctors—much to their gloom—may have finally gotten it right.

I know one more thing about her. She looks at her life today this way: The choices she was unable to make as a young woman of her time might have made her life more exciting and more visible. The ones she did make were good and durable and right for the time. Her husband, Oscar, built churches and Bible institutes from their native South Dakota to Minnesota to California and Norway. She spoke to a thousand church groups, study clubs, and kid banquets. Their Mark became one of the most respected ministers in Lutheranism, Joanne an executive of Lutheran Social Service, and Mary a schoolteacher in New England. For her husband's last fourteen years of life, she nursed him through Parkinson's.

Joanne Negstad, her first daughter, has two photos in her bedroom—one of her mother, taken years ago, and another of her own daughter at graduation. "They frame my own life as a woman," she said. "There's practically no limit now to what is available to my daughter. In my mother's youth, women walked within barriers. My own life has been a kind of bridge between the women of those two eras. But there's been one constant in my mother's life, the thing that guided her in experiencing the world around her."

She was talking about service and faith. But there's a rare quality some people have. It takes the idea of service a little beyond. You've seen them. People who have it are able to serve friends and strangers alike without pretense, to do it on impulse and creatively. Sometimes a little mischief gets in there. Myrtle Hanson does those things better than almost anybody I have ever known.

She had a practice she adopted. In a room, school, house, or church, she greeted all of her friends, but first she would find someone she didn't know. She would discover that person, and she would make a new friendship. She bought that white Toyota so she could introduce those people to her cookies, but she broke a leg last year and groaned because it was just too much to look at that unused Toyota sitting in the driveway, with miles to go.

The miles are running out. She says it's time now, that she doesn't just want to "rust out." I'm not quite sure it is time. I'll take what the doctors say about Myrtle, and multiply it by about three or four.

———

A few days before she died, Myrtle Hanson read her columnist-friend's account of her waning days and her earlier times. She expressed her appreciation with a mixture of English, Norwegian, and Latin, and with an offer to bake cookies. She never got back to her kitchen or to her hymnals, but she died a human being fulfilled, a personification of the good life according to the word she read and the faith she followed.

Eugene farrell

The judge walked out of his chambers at the end of the day and made his way judiciously to a lounge a few blocks away in downtown Minneapolis. It was the social parlor of his day's routine. Time for a drink for the judge.

Familiar faces appeared. Good times rolled.

He unwound and stayed for hours. He was companionable and free with his friendship. People gravitated to him. He had an instinctive heartiness, a gift for embracing and for including. Long rambling stories around the table stretched out the dinner. He drank. This time he didn't get soaked. Yet the next morning, for the first time in his life, the judge made a somber accounting of the night before. He summarized it with a silent question:

"What am I doing to myself?"

A few days later, after a more pained examination of the prime years of his life, Gene Farrell answered the question. He had become an alcoholic. Never mind that scores of times he sat on the bench, first as a municipal judge and then in the district courtrooms of Hennepin County, and tried to make sense of the alcoholism of the defendants in front of him. He'd dispensed wisdom, guiding them—but usually ordering them—to treatment centers and eventually into the lodge of Alcoholics Anonymous.

Subconsciously, the judge might have been talking to himself as well as to the defendant who stood before him. The two of them, in fact, could have been conspirators in the ancient exercise of evasion and denial.

And a few days later he sat drinking coffee with a man on whom he had once passed judgment in a drinking and driving case. The man had long since regained his sobriety. Now they reversed roles. He became the sponsor of the judge who had sentenced him, introducing him to the society of recovering alcoholics.

It happened twenty years ago. In a few weeks, Eugene Farrell of Baudette, Minnesota, of Patton's Third Army and Bastogne, of seventeen years as a lawyer and twenty-six years as a judge, finds three currents of an eventful life flowing together. He reaches his seventieth birthday, the retirement age on the district bench, and his twentieth year of sobriety.

The most accurate yardstick of his stewardship may be the roster of his well-wishers. His testimonial parties will include hundreds of men and women, some in absentia, who stood to be sentenced in his courtroom. Some of those people are now his friends. They will thank him, not necessarily for being generous or for being wise, but for trying to understand.

This is a man who, out of his robes, could be mistaken for a chummy gardener, trundling around a little overweight, a little squat, a little rakish in his goatee, needling his golfing pals and making no pretense of knowing a whole lot about humanity.

But he does.

The clan of judges is a grandma's quilt of personalities. It gives you scholars, loners, political hacks, decent folks, hams, career climbers, autocrats, and dedicated public servants. There have been lawyers on the district bench more scholarly than Gene Farrell the last twenty years, although he's a good lawyer. There have been very few who more deserve the title of judge in the essence of its meaning: one who reasons and explores and decides, using the law for direction and his good sense for judgment.

"What he gave to his years as a judge and to those who served with him was something precious," said Kevin Burke, the county's chief judge. "It was applying his common sense and patience to the most difficult kind of courtroom issues and trials. So often, the law is simply a guide. A man like Gene deepens it. He brings calm and knowledge of the human condition. I remember him telling me when we first met, 'Sometimes there are no really right decisions. Something is missing and it can't be found. You just have to be honest and decide it the best you can.' "

Lawyers are among the world's most relentless gossips: This judge is smart and that judge is a pushover for the woman's side in a divorce. That judge is a hairsplitter and this one is OK. Nobody who drew Farrell worried very much about a fair shot.

Lawyers worry about fairness on the bench as much as their clients do, but none of them worry with a man like Farrell up there. Mel Peterson, a lawyer, said: "This judge wasn't a handwringer about looking into the human side of a case. He just wanted to know how the rivals in a case or the defendants ticked. What's in a judge's guts is sometimes more important than what's in his or her head. That's the intuitive part of it. If that's sound, you have a judge."

This is a judge. One of his colleagues who meets the lawyers' test of a thoughtful judge, Gary Larson, looks at Farrell's recovery from alcoholism as something close to an act of grace in Farrell's professional life. It deepened his insights in the courtroom. He was able to take the spear-throwing parties in a domestic case and bring them to some semblance of mutual understanding. "He made recovery a cause," Larson said. "He's been a catalyst both in the courtroom and in his private life. That's a pretty wonderful life."

The judge from Baudette almost didn't get there. He took some shrapnel fighting in Patton's Third Army in the Battle of the Bulge, but finished law school and after private practice was appointed to the municipal court. He's never made a secret of his alcoholism and recovery. In court, in fact, he sees himself as a tool of the recovery process, a low-key evangelist who suggests to those he sentences that there's a better way than fried brains.

"When I look back I feel true humility in being in a place where I entered so many lives. It might have been traumatic for most of them. I tried to be compassionate, but I was also pretty rough on people who injured other people or refused to learn. I'm more appalled each day by the violence in our society—from broken families, from poverty, from meanness, and from too many guns. Yet there's been only one time when I looked into the eyes of a defendant and could not find a human. That was a fellow named Doughty who did something awful to a woman. I saw nothing. Everybody else, if you look deep enough you'll find something human, something good."

He'll play some golf for a while in Arizona, paint a little, write what he's sure will be bad poetry, and return for part-time courtroom chores. He'll also give a few socials. Bring your own mineral water.

Corey svien

The make-believes of Corey Svien's life were full of teddy bears and fictitious characters. They romped around in his childhood, the imaginary family of a dying boy.

He gave them names. But he didn't invent them to be his creatures of escape from pain and barriers. He gave them more than big eyes and charming snouts and coloring-book aliases.

He used them to speak to his friends, to his teachers, and to us. If the teddy bears in his journals and cartoon books made Corey Svien an ordinary Minneapolis boy, they were the only part of his life that was ordinary.

In his fourteen years that ended four days ago, he brought something profound and indefinable into the lives of hundreds of people. Some of them were doctors and nurses who were astonished by his grasp of the dynamics of hope and of dying and of reconciliation. Some of them were lonely, scared, and groping parents of kids with cancer, people who needed nothing as badly as a friend who knew. He gave them that.

He was a frail little evangelist, bald-headed part of the time, a needler some of the time, a healer almost always. Sometime after he lost a kidney to cancer, before he lost a lung to cancer, between his operations and chemotherapy, he found his mission.

Why is it that a dying kid can find a mission, can actually find a meaning in his life and a peace, when so many of us reach and flail for those? We can do it expensively or frantically or futilely.

There was nothing of that description in Corey Svien's fourteen years of life.

"He had a greater impact on patients around here than 90 percent of the doctors," said Dr. Bill Krivit of the University of Minnesota Hospital. "He was an adult in child's garments. He drew people to him. It was almost as though he could look beyond their eyes and into their minds and hearts."

He rarely did it solemnly. The last time he attended actor Paul Newman's camp for young cancer patients in Connecticut, he had his bald head painted with a mock message of warning to anyone who messed with Corey Svien: "Touch this head and die!"

You may have met him here nearly three years ago. His friend and patron at North Memorial Medical Center's Cancer Center, Tom Gacek, hustled some tickets for him and friends at a Vikings-Bears game in the Metrodome late in 1988. Corey found himself in the middle of a section reserved for Bears fans. For nearly two hours, he railed and chipped at the Bears fans with his crazy hat and T-shirt, and they threatened to throw him into the nacho cheese vat.

The Bears fans might have been a little gentler on him, after he danced a jig on their trampled hopes, if they had known he was watching his first pro football game between chemo sessions. He never told them. "It would have spoiled all of the fun," he said.

He had what the medical people called Wilms' tumor, a cancer of the kidney in children. He had very few years to live, which he must have known, but he also had a peace that came with the realization that he was needed. Therapists would call his gifts the skills of a networker. Idea marketers would call him a promoter. His idea was Coping with Cancer. It didn't mean that you necessarily would survive it indefinitely. It meant that you had to give yourself a chance. You had to hope and you had to live and you had to laugh.

This was just a school kid, fifty pounds, no more.

He went to Seward Elementary in south Minneapolis, but nothing he did there or anywhere else was easy. He came from a broken home and lived with his grandparents. When he was three, they removed a five-pound tumor. Gacek said that when he lifted his shirt, the scars and trenches in his body resembled a battlefield. You could wrap your thumb and forefinger around his ankles. He wore a sweat suit with a drawstring so he could use it to reinforce the belt on his pants, which were always hopelessly too large.

He built communities of kids with cancer and of their parents. He envisioned a support group made up of both kids and adults with cancer. Without wearing you out, he was a preacher. Sometimes, he grinned at his own intensities or his scrawniness.

He gave the names of teddy bears to some of his friends, and to himself. His pseudonym was Wiz Bear. It was easier sometimes to attribute serious ideas to a teddy bear rather than to himself, because eleven- and twelve-year-old kids aren't supposed to sound profound.

He defined some of his ideas in his writings, and in his talks. He defined them as a salesman. He promoted the turtles' race at the "U" hospital to raise money for cancer research. His ideas on how to expand the promotion popped out like jumping beans. They put him on committees with adults.

A few weeks ago, he rode with Gacek to spend a weekend in the Wisconsin woods. At a Holiday gas station early in the morning, they found just two people. The kid started talking to them. One of them was recovering from a brain tumor operation, and the other had lost a family member to leukemia.

"He learned that in five minutes," Gacek said. "In another five minutes, he was networking, and they all had trouble ending the conversation because it was the most important conversation they had all day."

A magnetic kid. Not a superhuman kid. A kid who knew about pain and hope.

"I used to have trouble with my feelings about cancer," he said. "What I want to do is help other kids with those feelings. Grown-ups and doctors know the right words. But sometimes a kid talking to a kid, for real, can explain it better because it makes you closer."

He told a man from the Paul Newman camp, "I don't draw a person as a teddy bear unless they are a teddy bear. I have to feel that their spirit is bright and caring. That's the only way. My teddy bears started in my imagination, but they are linked with reality—they are symbols for real friendship, for real fighting together. They are great knights and fighters. It can be the most horrible thing; they are going to defeat it. For me and my friends, the thing the teddy bears are fighting against is cancer." Some things can be defeated. Some cannot. Victory does not mean you are immortal. Victory means you gave what was in you, and you made those around you stronger.

By that definition, Corey Svien's life from its start to its finish four days ago, when the cancer spread into his remaining lung and pneumonia came on, was a victory. His heart stopped. His grandfather tried to revive him. They called 911, and he was taken to the hospital where he had made so many friends and converts, the university's. He died there.

"I can't explain why he has made me so much stronger," said Mary Hastings of the hospital's special projects division. "He did. He was a boy in so many ways, mischievous, wangling cash from the nurses and doctors so he could play his games. But he was a healer and a friend."

And still a child. A teddy bear sat in the room above his casket Monday. It didn't have a name. It might have been one of Corey's allegories. It represented all teddy bears, and the victory over darkness about which all teddy bears seem instinctively to know.

Charlie **brown**

The world saw him as a pie-faced little fellow with his baseball cap askew, sometimes looking harried, sometimes lost.

There was a kink of hair on Charlie Brown's forehead and in his eyes a trace of sadness, but more of fun and innocence and much that was good, and that is how he made the world feel. His face in the comic strip was a portrait of vulnerability and warmth. Because it was a believable portrait, it released us for a few moments each day from our tumult and clashes.

The man whose face and life inspired the cartoon Charlie Brown died at fifty-seven in the hospice at Metropolitan Medical Center. He was a man who trudged fallibly through life, grappling with his insecurities and manic depression and, for the last seven years, with cancer. But somehow he acquired hundreds of friends as he did so, because he was a good man at core, Charlie Brown, and that fact lit the places where he went and the people he met.

Charlie Brown never tried to conceal his failures. Subconsciously he tended to magnify them, his professional failures, his flops as a schoolboy athlete, the breakdown of some of the important relationships in his life. The irony for Charlie Brown was his inability to see in his dying years what an extraordinary success his life had become, in what it had overcome and his civility in doing it.

The young doctor who attended him in the later days of his illness marveled at what she'd seen in his final weeks.

"People just flocked to see him," Dr. Gail Bender said. "Usually it isn't that way. Most people don't like to expose themselves to death and dying. He lived through his pain and he found so much worthwhile that seemed to take him out of his pain. He was working on a book that he wanted to finish, but didn't quite make it. He poured into that a lot of the spirituality he acquired. But a few weeks ago he decided that his treatment had gone far enough, and it was time to die. I'll always remember his round face and smile.

"I think the scene I'll carry with me best is the one where I came across him accidentally one day while we were both heading for the hospital. He was driving his red convertible. The sun was out and the sky was blue and Charlie was grinning and just tickled to be alive at that moment."

He once thought he was an ugly little guy.

Not ugly in the visual sense but in how he worried about losing friendships, worried about where his alcoholism (which later subsided) was taking him, his psychological problems, and then his uneven career as a young artist.

He and the creator of the cartoon Charlie Brown, Charles Schulz, met in an art class at the Bureau of Engraving in Minneapolis. Schulz was attracted to his friendliness and the easy way he squelched himself for his blunders. Charles Schulz told of his plans to try to market a comic strip, and of a central character in it who struggled and tried to do well. He asked, could he call it "Good Old Charlie Brown"? Charlie saw a glimmer of approaching stardom there. He said, "Sure, of course."

The syndicate thought "Peanuts" would be shorter and better.

The characters in it and the values Charles Schulz invested in them eventually made Schulz and "Peanuts" a global conglomerate. The two Charlies were in touch almost to the end. People would ask Charlie Brown whether he was proud or excited about being famous, and he would ask them what had he done to deserve being famous, apart from being Charles Schulz's friend.

But when he finally found his way to the kind of human service his instincts prepared him for, being a program director for the

Hennepin County Juvenile Detention Center, he needed no artificial notoriety to justify Charlie Brown.

The young offenders he counseled gave him their gratitude, and some of them will be at his service. Maybe there were secret if harmless twists in his deepest personality that made him afraid of rejection, and maybe because of this Charlie Brown in later years threw himself into the idea of service.

It became another irony of his life. The fictional Charlie Brown entertained and instructed millions. The real Charlie Brown made troubled people strong in ways beyond the reach of the little cartoon figure that amused Charlie himself.

He healed them by going another mile and by caring, and by un-intentionally offering the evidence of himself: a very flawed human being who, because he didn't deny those imperfections and sought to grow out of them, gave hope to others more flawed.

He lived alone, never marrying, survived by a brother and sister who remember him best for the times he'd call when either was down and they'd finish their conversations in winds of laughter. Sometimes it's good to feel absurd and laugh your way out of your pain or preten-sions. He had gone through radical surgery for prostate cancer, then radiology. He lost his hair and avenged that by buying a reddish brown hairpiece that seemed to restore a little bit of the leprechaun in him.

"I think it would have made him laugh," his sister said, "to learn that somebody almost got the wrong day in giving the day of his service."

But if there is a way to understand a notion of "good grief," it's probably understood best by those who knew, and were made a little better by, Charlie Brown.

music in their lives

Rosa bogar

A woman from the suburbs telephoned with an announcement: "I've just met this remarkable black woman. She designs fantastic clothes and writes poetry and everything she does and says seems to have music in it."

Rosa, I said.

"You know her?"

Yes and no. When I hear Rosa's voice I get the same sensations I feel when I open the lid to my favorite music box. The sound summons something good and familiar and confidential. Yet it's always far enough away to be elusive. Rosa calls every four or five months to talk about poetry and her life. She talks about how she picked cotton in South Carolina when she was a kid, and how at fourteen she wrote poetry that was innocent but laced with so much erotic whimsy it convinced her mother that she was doing something awful.

"I wasn't," Rosa says. "I didn't even take the idea of boys seriously. But we were poor. I had twelve brothers and sisters. We couldn't go anywhere. So I traveled with my mind. I went to strange and incredible places. I imagined all of it and I put it on paper, just flowing free, and I scared my mother almost to death."

We are locked on the same frequency as telephone pals. I've seen Rosa Bogar only once. We banter and needle and say silly things on the phone because we enjoy the conversation, but I prolong it for reasons that may be entirely selfish: It is hard to resist the lyrical leaps and flitting of Rosa's mind.

"I feel like a tree," she told me not long ago. "I'm pretty tall and I feel loose and I like to swing my arms in the breeze, but I've never figured out what kind of tree I should be."

I told her she should consider being a willow.

"Well, I like that," she said. "Willows are the kind of trees you feel you know and can meet."

Rosa Willow.

I told her my agents had reported her latest fashion success at the meeting of the Golden Valley Women's Club. Rosa is forty-eight, a woman who raised two sons, lives in north Minneapolis, and works as a paraprofessional at the Wilder Fundamentals school for grades kindergarten through six. This month, Black History Month, is a big deal for Rosa Bogar. Her promotional skills are mischievous but pretty relentless. She wanted a forum for her styles, which she calls "Free to Be." A friend got her invited to the Golden Valley gathering. Nearly ten years ago she published a book of her poetry called *Black Woman Sorrow*, in which her griefs and hidden longings, her awe and foolishness and pride tumbled out in the style of a minstrel singing the mixed ballads of life. But if poetry was her confession, the sewing machine was her Arabian carpet. She began making clothes and showing them wherever people were willing to look at them.

"They were totally original," said Nancy Smith of the Golden Valley women. "I don't know what part of her culture she was expressing in those clothes, but these particular ones were all worn by white women, and they just worked and they worked fabulously. She had one outfit in brilliant yellow, a cape and a skirt that became a double skirt, and there was one garment that worked either as a cape or a skirt, and the whole thing seemed just full of harmony."

How did a cotton picker become a designer, Rosa?

"I don't know if I'm a designer. I just make clothes. I can't market them. I don't have the money. But making them is something that goes all the way back to the cotton fields. Making something on my sewing machine excites me.

"Sometimes I get up in the middle of the night when I have an idea. I don't have any patterns. I don't use a tape. I always keep at least one piece of fabric around for those times in the middle of the night. I look at the fabric as something lying around pretty dead, until you have an idea, and then it comes alive and people can wear it, and you have given that piece of dead cloth some meaning and some joy. I make them free and loose so people of different sizes could wear them. Let's all have fun."

She picked cotton only on Saturdays when she was a girl. That way she could buy fabric for her creations and tuck them away in her head while she was picking cotton.

"I never learned the technique of picking cotton, like 'pick on your knees to save your back' and 'pick with both hands at the same time so you can pick more cotton.' I prayed for rain a lot so we could not pick cotton. If we were already in the field when rain started, we were taken home because cotton weighed more when it was wet and the 'cotton pick'n man,' which is what they called the manager, would be on the losing end when the cotton dried. I could never understand why the owners of the cotton fields were called the 'cotton pick'n man' when the field hands did all the picking."

She moved to Syracuse, New York, and then to Minneapolis, volunteered for this and that, made herself indispensable here and there, worked with kids in school who needed special attention, won a Martin Luther King prize a year ago for the tireless and innovative ways she has brought the races a little closer together. She remembers her poverty and the slights and humiliations she absorbed. Sometimes a forgivable response to this kind of treatment is bitterness.

It is not the way she has lived. You can be a victim and eventually win. You can be poor and still bring the harmonies or mirth of your inner life, your secret life, to a world that may not fully understand them.

A few days ago, kids asked me to name some of the great black heroes and memorable people as part of their exercise in Black History Month. I named most of the usual ones that a scarcely qualified nonblack will name, and some of the current ones. I also named Rosa Willow Bogar, whom I've met only once.

If you want the truth, I put her near the top of the list.

Jimmy bowman

When Jimmy Bowman played the piano, there was always a little less harm in the world. The night mellowed. If you were sitting at a supper club table, you were tempted to call a waiter to light the candle.

Jimmy's music created those atmospherics. When he played Duke Ellington and Cole Porter, his frolicking fingers came together with his mind and mustached grin. It was a perfect montage of ease and artistry.

The last place I saw him was in the lounge of J.P. Mulligan's in Plymouth. He sang a piece by Johnny Mercer, "Here's to My Lady," supporting it with a few chords and counterpoint here and there, pensive stuff, intimate but still with the required dash of sophistication. Just before his break he spotted an old acquaintance sitting at a table and came over.

I didn't tell him what I wanted to.

I'm no clairvoyant and there was no reason to believe Jimmy Bowman would be gone in two months. But it had been years since I'd last heard him and there was something in the air that made a summing-up seem right. Diners were chattering around us. Somebody let in a basketball game on the overhead TV, and suddenly it wasn't right.

So I told his son Thursday, the day after Jimmy died in a hospital at the age of 74.

"Hundreds of people knew your father far better than I did," I said, "but in the days when I met him, white people and black people had a hard time talking to each other, reacting to each other easily.

Doing it with affection was even harder. A lot of them still have that trouble, but more so then. Your father was the first black man who seemed to have reason to call me a friend. And when we talked we didn't have to do it with any elaborate courtesies or strained shows of attention.

"We just gabbed about music and ball. I used to ask him about Earl (Fatha) Hines and Billy Eckstine and Sarah Vaughan, people he had worked with, and he was almost adolescent in wanting to know the inside about jocks I covered, Fran Tarkenton and people like that.

"I don't know how this sounds to you, but we once shared dinner. It was the first time I'd done this with a black man. That's how deep the gulfs were in those days. He talked about his life, and here was this gifted, lighthearted piano player describing humiliation and triumph. He talked about struggle and then getting it on, and he made it all sound much less than the American saga that it was."

It was that, though. Jimmy Bowman, a postal worker's son from Louisiana, the class president at Fisk University in Tennessee, a second lieutenant in the infantry in World War II, almost killed in the explosion of a land mine beneath a tank in France. And then after all that, a year after the war he was ordered by a bus driver in Texas to step back because he was standing too close to the white seats.

An MP intervened, apologizing that "this is the way it has to be."

But a wounded veteran who was black could still make a good living if he got away from those buses and found something he could do better than most. Not many people played and sang romantic jazz with quite the same off-the-cuff elegance as Jimmy. His voice was light as down. He didn't do any tour de force. He romped and flitted, but once in a while he got into a reverie that came a little closer to soul.

Black musicians sometimes grumbled about Jimmy. They weren't sure his stuff was black enough. He got a lot of bookings from clubs that weren't interested in other black musicians. He listened to the grumblers and tried to be their broker. He was hardly an outsider as the victim of Jim Crow.

"My dad used to talk about the early days," Jimmy Jr. said. "After he played with Earl Hines for a while, he got club dates in Chicago. In those years the Mafia ran most of the clubs. Sometimes they paid the musicians. When they paid, they paid well. Sometimes they decided not to pay the musicians. When the musicians asked for the money, the Mafia characters just got out one of these big guns about the size of a howitzer. My dad got that treatment more than once."

It might have been often enough to send him to Minneapolis with his wife, Magdalene, Jimmy Jr., and his stepson, Mickey, back in the 1950s. Solo or with combos, he played in almost all of the major clubs in the Twin Cities and on the minnow-and-minigolf circuit of the northern lake resorts. In the south Minneapolis home where he lived with his family for the thirty-five years that ended two days ago, Jimmy's houseguest list would have stretched the eyeballs of jazz aficionados. Earl Hines often dropped in, Ike Cole and others.

"If you messed with drugs, though, you weren't on the list," his son said. "My dad was a pretty straight arrow. He played and sang and although he made it look easy, he was disciplined about how he did it. He played golf all the time, and he did that well. With us he was a friend as much as a father. He was bouncy and kind but he set you straight about how you should treat others. Color didn't matter on that count. What you thought of yourself was important. He was open and fun, and when he ran into really rank racism, he seemed more sad than mad. He thought people had come further."

Who knows how far, if very far at all, people have come?

His life was good and full because he brought to it not only uncommon gifts but a willingness to understand ignorance and not be poisoned by it. He served thousands of people with his music. He served others, including one who shared his dinner once, with his buoyant goodwill and his sensible grasp of what matters in life.

It is something to remember about Jimmy when his peers in jazz play some of the music he liked best at his service. He always played beautifully.

He may have taught life even better.

Alexander toradze

Mother, never mind buying ice skates and secondhand Toyotas to relieve your guilt pangs about the kid's future. Buy the kid a piano. You don't need a piano with a Viennese pedigree. A retread from the want ads with two wobbly black keys will do.

If you have a piano, concoct whatever ruse seems civilized to get the kid into lessons. Flattery is OK. Immunity from grounding may be more practical. Extortion and bribery are permissible.

The trade-off could be immense. I'm telling you this seriously. I do that after watching hundreds of mature, sensible people—many of them forced into that condition by their Scandinavian genes—come totally unstrung by a piano player who walked onto the stage looking like a man just drafted as a nose tackle by the Detroit Lions.

What happened in the next hour should change your mind about the best way to make your kid irresistible and needed by the masses. It may be the one sure way to give your kid the three minimal rewards the kid's brilliance deserves from today's world: wealth, adoration, and unlimited medical benefits.

Most modern mothers try to achieve these goals by raising their children to be tight ends or TV meteorologists. After spending the noon hour at Orchestra Hall Thursday, I say this is a mistake. Your child could be another Alexander Toradze. I admit this might take some ingenuity. Toradze was born in Georgia in the former Soviet Union and plays the piano with the clashing passions of a blacksmith who discovers the joys of growing gladioli.

I don't know any tight ends with that kind of virtuosity.

Years ago my venerable pal, Barbara Flanagan, mounted a campaign to give performing artists in town the same attention we give to athletes and polar explorers. The idea is that a symphony conductor such as Edo de Waart, for example, is a lot more interesting, higher paid, and certainly more venturesome maritally than Tom Kelly or Kirk Lowdermilk. Who could deny it? The scheme never caught on. Too bad. There are still more people in town who remember Bombo Rivera, the frantic outfielder, than Rhadames Angelucci, the oboe player.

But times are on the move. Pavarotti makes the newspapers as often as Magic Johnson, although Pavarotti is badly outreached and could never handle a jump ball. But neither of the two, I'm telling you solemnly, could touch Alexander Toradze in the raw electricity he generated at Orchestra Hall. Mother, you should have been there. It would have changed forever your picture of your son's or daughter's arrival as a global concert star. This was no manikin in a tux and cummerbund. This was a gorilla with misty eyes. He played Rachmaninoff with feathers and fists. He was less than halfway through the first movement of Rachmaninoff's Third Piano Concerto, and most of the audience had voluntarily stopped breathing to watch the action.

Most good piano players cannot play Rachmaninoff's Third Piano Concerto, and, in fact, refuse to attempt it. Playing it is the musical counterpart of walking up the wall of a skyscraper in a hailstorm without ropes or suction cups. In other words, it is an almost impossible feat physically. But in the hands of a master pianist it takes the listener into wildly mixed emotional terrain, marbled with thunderbolts, melancholy, sweetness, longing, and plain and simple Slavic fatalism and romance.

All of that is Rachmaninoff. Folks at Orchestra Hall were expecting that. But they couldn't have been expecting what they got from Toradze. He came striding and rolling onto the stage in front of the conductor like a man who seemed more prepared for "The Beer Barrel

Polka" than Rachmaninoff. You could almost hear the seams of his blue suit coat splitting at his weight lifter's shoulders. His fingers looked like sausages. He was jowly and thick, but he seemed sociably modest and likable, and then, mother, he sat down to play.

In ten minutes you could hear good and restrained Scandinavian gasps from deep under those dice cubes in the auditorium. He played with violence and in reverie. He devoured the piano and he embraced it. Rachmaninoff's chords need a hand spread that amounts to a wingspan. When Rachmaninoff unleashes the full power of his racing chords, there is nothing in piano music to equal it in tumult and fury. Most musicians who try to play it are simply hanging on by then. Toradze took it at full charge. Sweat poured off his forehead. During the orchestral passages he grabbed for his mopping cloth. Then he was surging over the keyboard again with his shoulders, hands, and perspiration, and when the music turned from turbulence to tinkling banter, he hunched and cuddled the keys. He might have been petting a gerbil.

Critical purists balk at some of this. They say you can have passion and involvement without having theatrics, and I suppose when the guy got so involved that he played three bars standing up, that might be called theatrical.

But mother, raise your kid to be a Toradze instead of a Troy Aikman. This wasn't theatrical. The man was flat-out into it. He is going to last longer than Aikman. The job is safer. He doesn't have to worry about charley horses and homicidal linebackers. The piano doesn't blitz. Rachmaninoff's Third is not a contest, unless you count the last thirty-two bars of the finale, where the miracle was that everybody finished together.

But nobody finished like the Georgian blacksmith. He came churning down the keyboard while De Waart rode the orchestra into the galloping exit. And when Toradze hit the last chord, he leaped up massively and almost pitched himself into de Waart's lap, which was hard to do since the conductor was standing up and was outweighed by at least four stone.

Mother, the audience went nuts, unapologetically nuts.

No one is going to get that kind of reception at the ball game in Pasadena on Sunday. I don't think St. Peter would get it in the Vatican.

Check those piano want ads.

the entrepreneurs

Jeno paulucci

We're going to hear a minority report today in the latest Twin Cities airport scheme. Don't tell me you don't want to hear it. You can turn up the fan and run the dishwasher. You're still going to hear it.

Passing freight trains and overhead jets could not snuff out this minority report. When Jeno Paulucci talks, the normal rules of sound are revoked. Paulucci functions naturally in an atmosphere of pandemonium. His style is to jump in uninvited. When there's no pandemonium to intrude on, Paulucci creates it.

"The place for that airport is in Pine County, halfway between the Twin Cities and Duluth," Paulucci said. "I've been trying to convince the deadheads in Minneapolis and St. Paul of that for years. Now they want to waste billions of dollars putting a new airport near Hastings. Where's Hastings? The only thing I know about Hastings is it's on the way to the Mayo Clinic. That's good. That makes it convenient to do lobotomies on all the dummies who want to put an airport near Hastings."

I've devoted reasonable time over the years to trying to decode Jeno's version of simple math. It's expressed in the Paulucci Principle: The best way to get to Minneapolis is to fly seventy-five miles past Minneapolis.

Dozens of times I have asked Paulucci to explain this trail-blazing equation. Each time I come away freshly amazed. That's because of Jeno's original method of doing business. Although Paulucci's current net worth is approaching $1 billion, he shuns calculators and what he considers an even more obnoxious invention, the company financial officer. He is the only millionaire I've ever met who still does his corporate budgets by removing his socks to free his toes for the more intricate counting.

Because we're both natives of the Iron Range, Jeno adopts an attitude of forgiveness in the face of my mental paralysis when he talks about a global airport in Pine County, Minnesota. The others he dismisses with the usual eruptions of scorn and four-letter words. I get off easier. Consider his generous response the last time we argued about it. "You poor, dumb misguided packsack," he said. "This is how it comes down: You build another airport in the Twin Cities area and you compound the highway mess. One way or another, you're going to get choked. Either you get choked by the traffic or you get choked with taxes and fees and add-ons.

"Put an airport in Pine County and serve it with fast rail transit like the Japanese do, maybe up to 200 miles an hour. It's coming to all of the industrialized countries. It's inevitable. You'll have a Global Airport Center that will be a boon to northern Minnesota, as well as the Twin Cities and places to the south. You could fly from Atlanta and land in Pine County. An hour later you'd be in the Mayo Clinic or the Metrodome or Grandma's in Duluth."

I examined these options and thought I had a sensible question. Why would anybody fly from Atlanta to Pine County to go to Grandma's in Duluth?

"Because my son Mickey owns it, dummy. A Minnesota international airport should look at the big picture of Minnesota. It's a great place, great medicine, industry, nature, and education. Minnesota's health plan right now is better than you're going to get out of Congress. Northern Minnesota has tremendous resources itself. There's Duluth, the North Shore of Lake Superior, the Boundary Waters, the Iron Range. It has original thinking and practically an original language. It has practically no crime."

No crime?

"How many bank robbers do you know who make their getaways on a snowmobile?"

Paulucci made his money on Chinese food, Italian food, Florida real estate, and raw gall. He says most of the legends about him are true. He opened a can of his freshly made chow mein to share the ambrosia with potential underwriters. He found a dead grasshopper on top of the heap and, concealing his find beneath sighs of anticipated ecstasy, he swallowed the grasshopper and noodles in one swoop. He got the order. He also got indigestion. When a bigshot Hollywood ad writer, Stan Freberg, was late with one of Jeno's commercials and was stonewalling Paulucci's phone calls, Jeno hired a skywriter to ask where the hell was his ad. An unexpected southwest wind screwed up his ultimatum and turned it into a passing cloud. He once got upset when a columnist demanded that he should explain why he welched on a deal to buy a baseball club. Paulucci hired a charter plane to send me a sizzling five-page answer. He couldn't wait for the U.S. mail.

Although he still employs an estimated 600 people in Duluth, he moved most of his operations to Florida, supposedly to build new empires. That is a myth. Paulucci left Duluth mostly because he wanted to use steel-studded snow tires to fight off winter in Duluth. The ordinances said that was illegal. Paulucci told them to change the ordinances. They didn't, so he left.

People elsewhere look on Paulucci with a mixture of awe and astonishment. Those attitudes never show on the Iron Range. For years, Paulucci has been trying to reopen a plant on the Range to reestablish his roots. When his proposal comes before the Range councils, Paulucci and the politicians accuse each other of ingratitude. They end up not speaking to each other, which is the best therapy for both.

Paulucci isn't an airport commissioner here or in Florida. At seventy-five he's now invading Japan with his lines of Italian food, Swedish meatballs, and whatever sells. He still goes to work at 5 A.M. and often on Sundays. His wife thinks he's sick when he doesn't. His airport

proposal is a minority report because he considers anybody with brains
to be in the minority in locating a new airport site in Minnesota.

Paulucci has not threatened to sue dummies or rival pizza-roll hawkers
recently, but it's early in the year. He once threatened to sue a small-
town editor who called him an Italian meatball. He said that being called
a meatball he could handle, but the other was an ethnic slur.

Nobody is spared Paulucci's eruptions when his tender genes are
touched. Bill Clinton took a full blast a couple of years before he got
elected. The provocation was Gennifer Flowers' version of her alleged
sexual liaisons and conversations with Clinton. They included his asides
about Governor Mario Cuomo of New York. Cuomo, Clinton told
the woman, acted like a Mafia figure and was a "mean son of a bitch."

Clinton didn't deny the references to Cuomo, although a few days
later he made what was described as an apology. Paulucci rarely ac-
cepts apologies. He prefers the transgressor's heart on a long spike.
The only time Jeno measures his words, he does it with a Richter scale.
So Jeno put on his robes of statesmanship and replied to Clinton in
his most reserved language:

"Over the years, we have had a lot of donkeys trying to kick down
the White House door, but until now, never a smart ass with a loose
tongue . . . It degrades not only Governor Cuomo by comparing him
to a mafioso but also insults the entire Italian-American community
of 25 million people . . . Clinton has to be a genetic fluke. He's got to
have five feet, all of which he put into his mouth at once with that
crack about Cuomo. I called my old friend, Walter Mondale. I told
him 1992 was the year to run for president. I told him I'd hold his
coat. He said he thought he had a schedule conflict."

Although he leads a half dozen Italian-American groups, Paulucci
usually lets history talk for the Italian culture and people. "What are
the cornerstones of today's civilization?" he once asked. All right, what?
"Music, art, and pizza. Remove the Italian contributions to those, and
what do you have?"

That's only three cornerstones.

He said he thought the fourth was so self-evident he didn't have to say it: Where would civilized lovemaking be today if it weren't for the Italians?

I thought we learned our lovemaking and nose rubbing from the Eskimos.

———————

A friend called Jeno Paulucci in the spring of 1995, inquiring about Jeno's plans for retirement, since Jeno was obviously a prudent man, who recognized his seventies as a time to throttle down. The caller got a thundering ten-minute lecture on the pitfalls of sloth and self-coddling, some of it printable, and was told a strong letter would follow. Jeno still runs his empire from Florida—Italian food and real estate— is credited with a net worth of $500 million, still conducts some of his business from Duluth, and still swings haymakers at Minnesota politicians and bureaucrats when they don't agree with him.

Stan mayslack

Millionaires cowered in his serving line. Truck drivers approached meekly and mute. When you walked through Stan Mayslack's buffet line, you fixed your eyes in the mandatory look of humility and kept your mouth shut.

The only sounds were the shuffling of feet and a dictatorial growl from Mayslack. He stood behind trays of roast beef in his intimidating beard and butcher's apron, piling slab after slab onto the paper platter of the obedient customer.

"It's heavy. Keep both hands on the plate, mister, or you could walk out of here with a broken wrist."

Nobody argued. He winked, barely. Original thinking was discouraged in the more than thirty years that Stan Mayslack offered his roast beef lunches at Mayslack's Polka Lounge in northeast Minneapolis. For hushed compliance, Mayslack's luncheon queues displayed the most distinctive qualities of a prison lineup.

Never mind that it was partly an act. Mayslack was a showman, a Polish posturer, a former pro wrestler who was part glowering autocrat and part mischief-maker. All right, he still is. But Monday he yielded to his seventy-eight years and the advice of his wife and brokers and disclosed the sale of Mayslack's Polka Lounge, ending a two-year search for a worthy successor.

Losing Memorial Stadium can be dealt with. So can the auctioning of the State Fair carousel. But northeast Minneapolis without Mayslack demands an instant outpouring of mourning. Hysterical grief is also acceptable.

I didn't say Mayslack is vanishing into history on the spot. At 290 pounds, still a few pounds below his best carving weight, Mayslack doesn't vanish easily. For a few months this winter he will preside as chef emeritus and serving-line maharajah to cushion the shock of customers while they get used to the new owner. Valentine Mus, another Northeasterner, plans to continue the Mayslack roast beef sandwich buffet. He will use the original recipe, which Mayslack has refused to divulge for more than three decades.

"It's time for Mayslack to create a legacy," the pasha said yesterday. "I'm giving the marinated beef recipe to the new owner. He has to provide his own cigar box to collect the money."

For years Mayslack's elfin, white-haired mother-in-law gathered the noon receipts in a cigar box at the end of the serving line. Mayslack would lecture gruffly to male customers on proper etiquette at the buffet table but roguishly squeeze the thumbs of female customers. He regarded himself as the embodiment of Old World courtliness. As such, he tried to break up an argument between two women several years ago. He explained that there had to be some middle ground where people of good will could come together.

"One of them hauled off and hammered me in the nose with her fist," Mayslack said. "It was a better blow than some I took in the ring."

Mayslack's Polka Lounge, with its venerable tile floor, stolid booths, and speakeasy aura, has resisted progress and countercultures with equal ease. Mayslack and Butch, his wife, bought it for $80,000 in 1955 and within a year installed the roast beef luncheon, which ultimately drew customers in packs. They wound a block down the street while clarinet trills from Polish love ballads on the jukebox skirled among roast beef feasters inside. Mayslack's clientele at the height of his business included the full spectrum of American society, from construction hard hats to Lake Minnetonka dowagers.

I told him one year he had to diversify culturally. "There is life after polka bands," I said. "The Harvard Glee Club is coming to town.

Invite the glee club to sing at Mayslack's." Mayslack at first declined. He thought the Harvard Glee Club was a team of rowers who competed in the Poughkeepsie Regatta. But they came in black tie and sang for two hours while tears streamed down the cheeks of bankers and corporate lawyers, Harvard old grads all, and into the stacks of roast beef filling their paper platters.

Mayslack wrestled professionally for thirty years, the latter part as the designated villain. He had dropped out of school in eighth grade to bring money into his family living in northeast Minneapolis. Before that he went daily to the train yards with other kids to pick coal out of railroad cars delivering to the Northern States Power plant. "I also went around with threshing crews, and I found a farmers' magazine where there was an article telling you how to wrestle. So I started wrestling."

Fundamentally, though, Mayslack is a promoter. He made himself rich promoting his densely spiced roast beef sandwich into an institution and promoting oddball New Year's parties at his polka lounge—Chinese and Russian New Year's, Mother's Day festivals, St. Patrick's Day parties with a Polish spin. One year I telephoned Mayslack from Winner, South Dakota, where I was reporting on a buffalo auction.

"Mayslack," I said, "I just bought you a half a buffalo to make buffalo burgers. It will be sensational." I gave Mayslack the price by phone, and he howled so fiercely it was nearly a disconnect. But he took delivery and made more than $1,000 in profits at one sitting two weeks later.

So I talked to him again yesterday, thanked him for his years of labor and service. I conveyed my respects to Butch, and said that since we were such close friends it was OK to confide his roast beef recipe.

"What am I, some kind of patsy?" he said. "I'll tell you what I use. I take a fifty-five-pound or fifty-eight-pound round of beef from Swanson's Meats on Lake Street and lace it with garlic, paprika, celery salt, more garlic, oregano, onions, and pepper. Did I forget garlic? I use twenty-five pounds of garlic a week. There is nothing that can't be solved with a little garlic. I call garlic buds Polish apples. I marinate the beef in white wine and put it in foil for eight hours at about 375 degrees.

"Outside of that, I'm not saying a thing. It's the loving care that makes the difference. I'm not going to look forward to going. Do you know what this place has meant to me? It's been fantastic. There is no place in the world like northeast Minneapolis and all those nationalities. I'm proud to be Polish. My wife, Butch, she was a Strzelecki. Our boy, Dick, is an analyst with Control Data. We've been married for fifty-two years, and we've done this together. She's not feeling the greatest right now, so it's best we leave the business.

"The place isn't going to change that much. They're going to keep our polka bands around. We rotate. We've got John Filipczak and the Classics and Bill Jerniak and Wee Willie. Don't ask me what Wee Willie's last name is. Am I some kind of music critic? No, he's not Polish. He's something half and half."

Mayslack railed on. He and Butch are a huge piece of northeast Minneapolis, beyond value, beyond succession. The Northeast of Stash and Butch is the Northeast of the unexpurgated Old World names and traditions, its struggles, prides, polka parties, three-day wedding blowouts, tempers, and devotion to family. They are going to give Stan and Butch one final party sometime down the road. They will send honorary invitations to people like Mitch Miller and Mary Tyler Moore, who have tried to outlast those huge roast beef sandwiches and never quite managed.

If you show up, rejoice and sing Polish—but keep both hands on the plate.

———

Stan Mayslack died in his sleep in February 1995 at the age of 84 in his apartment above the polka lounge where he presided for so many years as chef, host, and (occasionally) benevolent dictator. Butch, his wife of fifty-six years, died a year earlier. At Stan's request, Father Frank Perkovich, the polka mass priest from northern Minnesota, celebrated the requiem mass for Stan's funeral at Holy Cross Church, where he'd worshipped for most of his life.

Sid hartman

There stood Joe Namath in the middle of the shower after the ball game. He looked ferocious. He looked defiant. No mortal need approach.

Journalists, certainly the most mortal of the species, stayed away in hordes. They did not take this action out of courtesy. They did it in raw terror. Men who had faced hand grenades and artillery in wartime cowered. Namath could look mean squeezing a bar of Sweetheart Soap. To the seekers of truth carrying their notepads and recorders, the message was clear. Go home. If you want to talk, talk to the Hungarian field goal kicker. If you can't talk Hungarian, the readers are ahead.

But now there was movement in the demoralized press corps. A tall man carrying a tape recorder, a microphone, and a squeegee walked out of the mess and into the shower room.

Purposefully he sloshed toward the deluge. Namath turned and spotted him. He recognized him. Who wouldn't? The man was now taking water in his two-tone street shoes at an alarming rate, and the spray from Namath's shower had already wilted his shirt and drenched his hair. But there was no mistaking this oncoming merman. It was Sid Hartman, the unsinkable sports genius from Minnehaha Falls.

A half hour after Namath's Jets had demolished Fran Tarkenton's Giants in the Yale Bowl, Hartman was prepared to score one more breakthrough in a career fraught with scoops. He was going to perform the first underwater interview in the history of sportswriting. It wasn't because he was brave. Desperation almost always triumphs over bravery. The issue was reputation, the preserving of a legend. Like the

Mounties, Sid always gets his man. Sooner or later, most of the sporting authors get stonewalled. Blanked. The Namaths will stare them down, ignore them, insult them, or take a thirty-minute shower.

Sid is impervious to insult and can be ignored only in the way Hurricane Hazel can be ignored. In getting a quote, he wields a bottomless arsenal of counterweapons. They include flattery, phone calls to the hero's hometown priest or bondsman, flattery, an iron will to match survivors of Stalingrad, and flattery.

In addition to the rest of his urgencies, Sid faced the threat of being blackballed by his cronies at the 620 Club if he came back without interviewing Joe Namath, one of his growing legion of close personal friends. An eyewitness to the scene was a longtime New England newspaperman who had covered both football and marine disasters. He said he'd never seen a performance to match Sid's in either field.

He was talking about both Sid's seamanship and his agility in avoiding a case of the bends.

"Sid was the only guy able to get close to Namath. You should have been here. There he was, walking fully clothed into the middle of the shower room. All five of the shower heads were going. There must have been fifty barrels of water a minute coming down. Actually, it was scary. One time, your man thought he stuck a microphone under the shower. He must have put the wrong hand out, because Namath started out talking to bar of soap. The rest of us stood around the drain trough. We were protected from the spray. Namath wouldn't give us the time of day. We thought of sending a guy in there with an umbrella. But he would have looked silly alongside your man, who was up to his socks in standing water.

"Sid had the standard tape recorder and microphone, but everybody was convinced he had some kind of snorkeling device attached. The roar of the shower was so strong that he had to get right in there with Namath. They stood head to head. It looked like Sid was trying to get an interview in the middle of Victoria Falls, which could have happened if he was after Mickey Mantle. Namath was barely visible in the clouds of steam. I'm sure he figured there was no way Sid could take notes with a ballpoint pen underwater, and he didn't think a guy with a recorder would risk electrocution just for a quote after an exhibition game."

But the sight of Sid wading toward him through the cascades obviously unnerved him. Namath may be tough enough to play through hangovers and sleepless nights, but the man's heart, after all, is not a slab of concrete. Sid's aquatic skills had to be rewarded. He gave the interview.

"Right," Namath yelled through the downpour, "this was our best game of the season. If Fran had my line it could have gone the other way. No, I don't know what the turning point was. For God's sake, Sid. Why do you want to know if I ever dreamed about playing in the Yale Bowl? You don't need that. What you need is a towel."

Or a resuscitator.

The interview ended, Namath dressed silently and left the rest of the press box crew grubbing in the soap trays for Sid's discarded tapes.

Give the man credit. He did it all without a life jacket.

Rebecca rand

Rebecca Rand's career has experienced more gripping moments than the phone call of condolence she got from the middle of Minnesota's potato plantations.

It came from an outdoor telephone booth next to the Cenex store in Argyle, Minnesota, which is roughly midway between St. Paul and the Harding Icefield of the Gulf of Alaska. I can tell you this because I placed the call. In fact, I HAVE to tell you this because, before I hung up, the news had spread across 15,000 acres of Red River Valley potato fields and was getting more local attention than the waves of weekend shoppers from Canada.

"Somebody called Rebecca Rand from Argyle."

That's correct. It may or may not have been a first. I called the madam with an apology. We were going to meet for lunch at Muffuletta in St. Paul to discuss her latest transgressions. In making the appointment, I forgot a previous commitment to meet with the book lovers of Hallock.

Hallock is reachable several ways, none of them easy. Hallock is an orderly and horizontal little city in extreme northwestern Minnesota, where a rumble strip on the highway constitutes a hill. It is nearly 400 miles from the Twin Cities, almost as distant as Chicago. Unfortunately, Northwest Airlines does not serve both cities. It does fly to Grand Forks, North Dakota, which is famed as the gateway to Hallock. At the Grand Forks terminal, I was greeted by Judy Vroom of the Hallock book lovers. She arrived with a station wagon, hot coffee, and battery-operated warm blankets.

At Argyle I asked her to stop the car. "I have to call Rebecca Rand," I said.

She asked whether I wanted privacy.

I said no, I doubt if there are many secrets in the potato fields.

She said I got that right.

I didn't call Rebecca Rand to philosophize. She says she can run a brothel if she wants to. The law says candidly that she can't. By way of reinforcing this judgment, the court produced some numbers at the end of the trial and handed them to the former madam: That'll be $200,000, two saunas, six months, and your little black book.

Rebecca is articulate, saucy, bright, and rich. The law says she is also illegal in the role of madam. She, in the words of the retired district judge Neil Riley, is "totally baffling." I asked the judge some time ago how is she baffling.

"Everybody who has watched her battle the bluenoses and the cops wants to reform her into something constructive because she's so smart and intriguing. She keeps on defying the law and riling the prosecutors and making money. But everybody has got a new mission they want Rebecca to take on, something sanitized and noble. It never quite appeals to her."

Friday, Rebecca offered one not previously nominated.

"When I get out of jail I may become a Wayzata housewife."

Well, now.

"It's an option. There's a man in my life who is marriageable. It could be one of the social events of the year in Wayzata. But philosophically it would be a pretty rough shock." It would also produce a pretty fascinating guest list.

People have been telling her for years that she would be a fireball as a lawyer, an occupation for which her daughter is studying.

"After this," she said, "I'd have to get a pardon, and I wouldn't want to start ordering textbooks waiting for that to happen. It's a dilemma for me. I liked what I was doing. But I'm going to come out on twenty years probation, which means I couldn't go back to what I do best until I was sixty-four. I like to travel and I could open a travel agency, but my notoriety is going to get in the way of every promotion I do. I could leave town."

That is an idea applauded by cops, prosecutors, and hundreds of antiprostitution activists, whose pressure had something to do with her latest bust and jail stretch.

"The climate is different," she admitted. "Years before, people would tell me: I don't like what you do but I like your independence. Now, the pressure against me is personal and hard."

For a long time, though, media folk found her hard to resist. She was talkative and outrageous. Sometimes she was hilarious. Because she made crates of money on prostitution, she could bid fancy prices on silent auction prizes that one year included a lunch with Governor Rudy Perpich and his wife. She drove up to the governor's mansion in a spiffy car with the vanity license plate of "Madam."

The governor tried his level best to be gallant. But he kept getting broccoli caught in his gulps, a condition rarely conducive to gallantry.

She accused society, the cops, and judges of hypocrisy in being tougher on an act of sex-for-money (which she seriously contends produces no victims) than they are on crimes she calls truly immoral, such as marketing schemes exploiting the poor and the dull.

And although she spent several stretches behind bars and was more familiar in court than the bailiff, she didn't repent her most recent encounter very fervently. The state nicked her for a lot of money, which, she said, tells her she should have hid it better. She once told an interviewer that she worked with a counselor for six months to learn as much as she could about her attitudes towards sex, whether they were healthy and open or compulsive.

"I came to the conclusion that there's value to fidelity and there's value to variety, and we have the right to choose which is right for us, and we have the right to change our opinion at various times as long as we're not dishonest or manipulative."

She added: "We both concluded that what I was doing was fine for me."

Nobody should be entirely shocked at that verdict.

But people who are her friends recognize now that Becky Rand, the Most Famous Madam in Minnesota, can't afford another bust. So they keep trying to move her into safe directions.

How about something revolutionary as a way out of the dilemma? How about a job, 8 to 5, for a bright and saucy woman nearing middle age, a job that requires no fingerprints or wiretaps?

"It would be awfully hard to take orders at this stage. Maybe I should go into volunteer work."

In the meantime, keep an eye on the Wayzata wedding announcements. It's early in the bafflement season.

———————

The ex-madam's lack of admiration for antiprostitution laws has not diminished since her return to mainstream society as a dutiful citizen. Approaching middle age, though, she decided she was not going to reform the country in her lifetime or win any prolonged wars with the government. Her domestic life with a retired businessman has been a success, she says. They travel, get involved in some social causes, and stay out of the strobe light. Her daughter, Lara, is now practicing law. "It's a shame Rebecca didn't go into law herself early in life," said Neil Riley, a former judge. "She would have won every case in sight."

the spellbinders

Miles lord

Two of the town's hotshot lawyers were locked in the usual pretrial impasse. It was a civil case and the argument was over the huge amounts of money their clients were demanding from each other.

It looked like at least two years squabbling and inaction ahead. The lawyers sighed. It was a tough way to pocket a half-million-dollar fee.

Both got a phone call to attend a court-arranged meeting in a downtown hotel. Shortly after they sat down, somebody knocked on the door. It was the bell captain bearing a six-pack of beer. With it came a message: The door was going to be locked. They could make the beer last as long as they wanted, but the door wouldn't be unlocked until they reached a settlement.

The beer and the ultimatum both arrived with the compliments of the Honorable Miles Lord, judge of U.S. district court.

According to accounts, the signed settlement and the six-pack finished in a dead heat. It took two hours.

Nobody has denied the account.

Miles Lord retired from the federal bench a few days ago. It was an act of chivalry to physicians, specifically to the ones who minister to the ulcers of all the appeals court judges who have tried to cope with Miles the past twenty years.

To his more sedate superiors, the judge has been a handful and a pain in their robed rear ends. His sins as a federal judge have been impressive. He has been noisy, prosecutorial, self-serving, and morally righteous in a way that kept rattling the ancient timbers of federal court tradition.

Purists will forgive me for not calling the judge by his last name. Almost no one who deals with Miles calls him anything but Miles. This includes lawyers, judges, journalists, and felons. It means the judge's saucy personality and courtroom style have made it impossible to duplicate him. For this, the republic should give thanks. Two Miles Lords might be the best argument there is for lynch justice. For better or worse, and sometimes both, Miles became an irreplaceable resource.

I say "worse" only because of the havoc the judge has spread with such relish on the historic role of the court. For good reasons, judges shouldn't be combative and partisan and use the bench as a stage for vendettas and social monologues.

This one has. The fact that he has and can still leave the federal bench under his own power says much for his durability, his friends, and his luck. It also says much for the system's safeguards against easy removal of a federal judge.

But he goes with the regrets of most people who know him. If he was a judicial ham, he was an enjoyable ham. If he went in for legal brawling, it was usually a fair fight. His targets were the economic powerhouses that he was convinced exploited customers and employees. When he got titans like that in his courtroom, he was less a judge than a pesky country lawyer lobbing rhetorical cow chips at the big shots.

He had most of them figured about right, otherwise he wouldn't have lasted as long as he did. Miles saw himself as a roughhousing Robin Hood defending the people's clean air and water, exposing the corporate manipulators, and offering the shelter of the court to the faceless little people who got ground up by big money and big government.

The court of appeals often saw him differently. He was a runaway cannon who had to be spiked for the dignity of the bench and the sanity of the appeals court.

Nobody should have been surprised by Miles's impatience with dignity. He was an alley fighter who grew up on the Cuyuna Iron Range of Minnesota. He was also a bellhop, a cat skinner, and a fry cook. He boxed in the Golden Gloves and got his prelaw training in economics by going broke trying to run a restaurant in Crosby-Ironton. As a college student he worked from 1 to 5 P.M. as a janitor, from 6 to 10 as a postal clerk, and from 11 P.M. to 7 A.M. as a night watchman. Someplace in there he attended classes often enough to get his law degree, which didn't impress his political pals nearly as much as his brass on the campaign road, where he nearly drove Hubert Humphrey out of his mind. Miles picked friends better than he cooked or boxed. With Humphrey and Orville Freeman, he was a ringleader in the Democratic-Farmer-Labor Party's emergence to power in the early 1950s. He got elected as the attorney general, but Humphrey went to his grave two decades later wondering how he did it.

He was the party cutup, a boisterous reformer who swung the populist's broadax and did it with the disposition of a hotfooter.

Humphrey and Lord were campaigning together in the 1950s when their small caravan encountered a bus carrying some senior citizens. Lord entered the bus first to do some casual electioneering. A few minutes later, Humphrey, already famous as a senator, clambered in with his customary grassroots glow. He prepared for a reunion with his longtime admirers, people he joyously addressed as "the soul of Minnesota."

Nobody gave him a tumble.

He worked both sides of the aisle diligently but to no avail. The elderly passengers ignored him unanimously. At the rear of the bus a dismayed Humphrey asked one of the citizens if he could explain the eruption of silence.

"You got a lot of nerve," the old one said. "We heard all about you. The young fella who was just in here said there'd be a guy coming on the bus impersonating Hubert Humphrey. He said give this guy the cold shoulder. The young fella said his name is Miles Lord. Real nice fella. I don't know who the hell YOU are."

But Humphrey, of course, carried no intramural grudges, because when a federal court vacancy came up in 1966, Lyndon Johnson was president, Humphrey was vice president—and Miles Lord was available.

Twenty years, Miles decided a few days ago, is about enough. It is a view probably shared by his critics. Critics don't influence the judge much. What influenced him more were his instincts. The political times have outrun his kind of rollicking populism and humanism on the federal bench.

If you had to put it to a vote, I'd say society is better today because Miles served on the bench. He took some of the shadier power of the mighty and brought it out into the sunlight. He wasn't always sustained. But he got their attention. And in some case, he got a hunk of their money for their victims.

He acted to preserve wilderness and clean air from the polluters. He did it imperfectly, and he didn't exactly shrink from taking a bow here and there. But he spoke with nerve and necessity, and he was a good and memorable judge for that.

None of the school yearbooks in which Miles Lord appears ever predicted that Miles would placidly disappear into the sunset when he became eligible for golden age discounts. He didn't. After Miles retired from the federal bench he moved into private practice, specializing in personal injury cases—"where the poor need the best advocate they can get." Miles modestly volunteered himself for this role. He shows no symptoms of total retirement.

Hubert humphrey

Most reputable pollsters believe Hubert Humphrey would have overtaken Richard Nixon in the 1968 presidential election if the campaign had lasted two or three days longer. A week before the election, Humphrey had dramatically reduced Nixon's lead and was charging hard in the final days. Why he found himself so far back in the early weeks may be explained in the piece that follows.

Humphrey is remembered today as the most popular figure in Minnesota political history. His voice and his legislation in the fields of health, in reversing the plight of the poor and minorities, and in education and human services made life better for millions in this country and around the world. He was a man of limitless energy and goodwill. He risked political oblivion by leading the liberal wing of the Democratic Party out of its traditional alliance with the Jim Crow politics of the South. He survived that—and the reputation of being a political loudmouth—to win the affection of millions.

He might have been president. But his campaign never completely recovered from a nightmarish episode in Seattle one Saturday night in the fall of 1968.

He stands at the speakers' podium, a man who would be president of the United States. He is prepared for the applause of thousands in the auditorium. Instead, as Lyndon Johnson's vice president, he hears himself called a warmonger, a murderer, and a racist. Posters depict him as the American Adolph Hitler.

The taunts and scorn hit Hubert Humphrey like a kick in the gut.

He glares into the balcony at a shaggy platoon of disrupters. His body language is intended to convey silent fury. What comes over is closer to disbelief. It seems to be saying, "Why me? Why do you want stick it to the best friend the poor and the neglected have got in this race? The best friend of peace. It's all in the record."

Later, he will say something close to that. But now he stands with his hands on his hips, looking wronged, distressed, and hapless—the Democratic candidate for president, unable to bring order to his own rally.

More than 10,000 party loyalists sit embarrassed and helpless. The protesters have a bullhorn and amplifying equipment, which they use to hold a mock arraignment. The scruffy prosecutors bring their charges, and nobody knows how to get rid of them.

It is a defining moment in Hubert Humphrey's campaign, one that may augur doom for it. Humphrey has been heckled before by young protesters of the war in Vietnam. But this was expected to be a triumphant Saturday night rally before a turnaway crowd, and it was counted on to send a bolt of electricity into a campaign that had been limping and discredited by party chaos, defeatism, and setbacks in the polls.

But what is happening, with Humphrey standing there absorbing the rowdy indictment, is closer to a horror. He tries reason and humor. From there he switches to eloquence and then to gentle talk, paternal chiding, and finally hard-eyed ridicule.

None of it works.

A half hour earlier he had entered the arena as the centerpiece of a tumultuous scene of blaring bands and clapping thousands, most of them working people and their families. It was a politician's Saturday night, a gala for the beaming Democrat who grew up in the tradition of Democratic-Farmer-Labor bean feeds and rollicking party blowouts in Minnesota. He had come to Seattle to deliver one of the first major addresses of his presidential campaign. Maybe now, he might have been saying, we're ready to roll.

Actor Gene Barry warms up the crowd with a song and a salute to Humphrey. The crowd wants to yell and have fun, and Humphrey senses it. Sitting in the front row behind the podium, he can barely restrain himself from leaping to the microphone. The crowd begins a chant: "We Want Humphrey."

"And you're going to get him," Barry shouts. With this he brings on the dialect comedian, Bill Dana, whose exact role on the program is not clear. But now the mood changes abruptly.

"Tell some of your Mexican-American jokes, you goddamned racist," one of the protestors yells down to the platform.

"Me, a racist?" Dana asks, incredulous. "Me, a Hungarian Jew?"

Dana begins fencing with them, asking to hear from a spokesman. But he's gradually losing ground. He wants to let them talk out their aggressions, to bring their abuse down on the platform before Humphrey speaks.

"End the war, end the war," a voice shouts. "Get the hell back to Los Angeles, you racist son of a bitch."

Dana speaks solemnly. "Hubert Humphrey will end the war for all of us," he says. "Hubert Horatio Humphrey was supporting the Negro, the Mexican-American, and the worker before you were born."

They jeer him down. There's a hatred and vehemence in the small gallery of protesters, and it will not be satisfied until its prime target is on his feet.

Sitting behind Dana, Humphrey crosses his arms on his chest and thrusts his jaw out, more out of injury than in defiance. He wants Dana to sit down, although he understands what the entertainer is trying to do.

Washington Senator Warren Magnuson comes on for a few minutes and then introduces Humphrey. Hubert walks to the microphone

smiling and waving. He has come to blast Richard Nixon, to lay down
challenges for a debate, and to draw him out on Vietnam.

But the raucous young galleryites don't let him get out of the gate.
"Stop the war," they scream. A kid with a long handlebar mustache
and elaborately sewn knee patches on his faded denim pants stands
and shouts: "Get out of here, you fascist bastard."

Humphrey turns from the podium to regard the gesturing youngsters, seemingly with good humor. He offers them time to speak. A
few voice standard antiwar slogans. But now a mousey brunette with a
frozen grin holds up a battery-operated loudspeaker. A bearded col-
league speaks into a microphone.

"In Vietnam, there's a scream that will not end," he begins.
Humphrey supporters start to shout him down. The candidate re-
strains them. "One set of bad manners is enough," he says. "We'll
keep quiet. We're going to let this fellow talk. Go ahead."

"In Vietnam, there's a wound that does not cease its bleeding . . .
We have not come to talk with you, Mr. Humphrey. We have come to
arrest you. We charge you with crimes against humanity. Stand before
the United Nations and the world and let them try you."

Humphrey is still waggish in the exchange. "Just be sure there's no
police brutality, that's all" (a reference to another of the protestors'
buzzwords, and an echo of the convention brawls in Chicago).

The gallery speaker sits down. Humphrey launches his speech.
But first he characterizes his tormentors. He says they are part of a
well-organized attempt to interrupt and embarrass him in his campaign. He calls it the tyranny of the minority. When the jeering breaks
out anew, Secret Service people move toward the protestors. Scuffling
breaks out. Some of the disrupters are moved toward the exits. Others
stay to listen. Free to talk, Humphrey starts in on Nixon. His speech is
crisp but mechanical. The candidate can't forget the spectacle of the
last half hour. He returns to it ad lib with a voice quavering and eyes
moist with emotion.

The protesters, he says, are driving thousands of voters into the arms of "another candidate who takes no stand." He finishes his talk and the crowd applauds earnestly. But the bean-feed camaraderie has been deadened. And the heavily guarded candidate returns to his hotel through the back door of the arena.

There is no landslide in sight tonight.

Walter mondale

There wasn't a wisp of an audience in sight when Fritz Mondale stepped off the curb on Eighth Street in Minneapolis and walked to the passenger side of a friend's compact.

Turning the door handle, he paused in the conditioned style of a politician ready to acknowledge passersby who recognized him. He looked bronzed and country-clubby in his expensive suit. If you want the truth, Fritz practically glowed. He could have walked out of the rising-aristocrat ads of *Fortune* magazine. If Ricardo Montalban didn't hold the long-term franchise for peddling Chryslers on television, Fritz would have gotten the job by acclamation. Here he stood, his carefully coiffed hair glistening in the dank gray of the spring morning. He beamed with self-assurance, and it didn't seem to molest his vibes that he was standing all alone.

Six months ago he caused traffic jams simply stepping out of the men's room. A presidential candidate in the middle of a campaign makes those waves.

Yesterday nobody saw him on Eighth Street. Well, let me correct that. I saw him. I would have slowed down to wave, but it occurred to me that this man has answered for enough consternation in the past six months without adding a bent fender to the damage.

Instead, seeing Mondale's tempered response to his personal catastrophe of the election—one state out of fifty, and that one barely— I let my thoughts drift to Ron Davis, the baseball pitcher.

Here is a man with a case of miseries that might seriously compete with a politician losing forty-nine states. Ron Davis is the Twins' relief pitcher, who is being paid a half million dollars for his current labors, which have now been transformed into throwing home-run balls in the ninth inning.

They interviewed him in New York Monday night in the middle of his latest gloom. It was provoked by a three-run homer by the Yankees' Don Mattingly. The odds that Davis could give up yet another game-losing home run in the ninth inning were pretty much beyond serious comprehension. Nonetheless, he defied the laws of chance and did it. Afterward he sank into the caves of self-flagellation, saying:

"I'm a disgrace. I can't keep screwing up like this . . . It's the lowest point in my life."

It struck me that Fritz Mondale may have learned something more than Ron Davis about where and how we locate ourselves in the universe.

Athletes and politicians are not so far removed from each other in the abnormal psychology of their daily worlds. They conduct their professional lives inside walls of glass, which can inflict all kinds of pain when they come crashing down. Both bring specialized skills to their trades, but they live ultimately for the electricity from the crowds. It's a giddy, dicey kind of existence. It exposes both the jock and the politician to a temptation—sometimes comic, sometimes tragic—to distort their identities.

The concentrated attention they get leads many of them to confuse who they are, meaning their worth as human beings, with what they do.

A lot of us make the same mistake with our own jobs or social roles, and when they end, suddenly there is isolation and self-abasement.

So here is this big galumping country boy willingly joining in all the scorn the failed ballplayer is supposed to deserve.

"I'm a disgrace."

Why? So he can't get his fastball past the good left-handed hitters anymore? Let his employers decide that. Should it be a character defect? If he can't get them out, he's not undermining his beer-drinking pals. It simply means he shouldn't be pitching any more. And when he can't, it doesn't mean he's a fungus on the family tree.

Mondale's debacle of 1984 might have been worse than a pitcher losing his fastball. I don't think he confused being a candidate for president with being Fritz Mondale. And that might explain his buoyancy on a gray day in spring six months later. Maybe we ought to consider how and why this particular politician dealt with the politician's most intimate grief.

Once in a while you'll find a public figure who becomes part of the comfort fabric of the environment in which he lives. He doesn't have to be lovable. He can be bland or slightly spacey. For the public, it comes down to this: When the politician defines the people he or she is talking to, and presumes to understand the recesses of their lives and hopes and quirks, do the people believe the politician? More, do they trust the politician?

Mondale is one who has gained that trust and held it. Which means this to the public: It's good and civilized having him around. That feeling is something you can't very well engineer. It depends on some fundamental qualities the politician brings to their table and lives: a good mind, intuitive good will, reliable decisions, a smattering of good luck, and a lot of wearability.

Walter Cronkite gives you that. And Mondale has brought those qualities to his public life. Republicans will feel slightly less proprietary about Mondale than the Democrats. But anybody's poll will reinforce his acceptability. Mondale is one of those bright apostles for a better life who came charging out of campus politics. He made a commitment to that mixture of sweat, gusto, revivalism that identified DFL politics in its early days. They never strayed very far from the farm and Main Street while they built their alliances with labor and the politically neglected. Those coalitions don't necessarily mean election in Minnesota or anyplace else. But they energized Mondale and lifted him to the higher reaches of his craft, although not quite the highest.

So a Fritz Mondale could tarry on a street in Minneapolis six months after the debacle, looking rested, ready to talk corn prices or the Twins' pitching, and notably short of devastation.

If there is life after a presidential election, Ron Davis, there certainly is life after two ninth-inning home runs.

For a harder fate than that, try campaigning as a liberal in downstate Illinois.

JIM KLOBUCHAR

Rudy perpich

Rudy Perpich came to the political battlefields with instincts as sure as his father's hands in the iron mines of the Mesabi.

That was the back-scenes wisdom in Minnesota politics. Until 1990, you couldn't argue with it. His instincts were right in 1982 when he charged into the Democratic-Farmer-Labor primary as the unsummoned Lone Ranger of Minnesota politics, won, and became governor. They were right in 1986 when he got reelected and in a dozen intraparty brawls stretching back to the mining country of his political cradle.

But they failed him in 1990, when practically everybody inside Minnesota politics could see the end coming except Rudy Perpich.

Someplace along the line, his instincts gave way to obsession: I'm the governor. They have to beat me.

The end was so visible that Arne Carlson was able to beat him with a campaign that lasted two weeks.

If that says something about Arne Carlson's ability to rise from the political dead, it might have said more about the blinders Perpich wore in his decision to run again.

He was a rollicking, popular character from the ore pits for most of his years in the political sun, and he earned that popularity. He gave the governor's job drive and a vision he never expressed very well but knew how to energize. He was full of mercurial impulses. He rushed off to visit voters in the dead of night, polka-danced with European duchesses, flew to a dozen faraway places to shop Minnesota's business and brains. He seemed astonished if the rest of the world was slow in

80

seeing something brilliant or irresistible about Minnesota. He brought a Super Bowl to Minnesota and nearly brought the Olympics. He also brought a chopsticks factory to the ore pits well before the Japanese and Chinese were ready to stake their futures and their egg rolls on Minnesota chopsticks.

He took risks and sometimes flopped. But he hit some notable ten-strikes, and he wore well until he got into media feuds over his family, his governing style, and his scattergun shifts in decisions. When Rudy felt misrepresented or unappreciated, his response was the miner's son's rather than a governor's. He said "to hell with you" and drove up to the Embarrass River, which might have been symbolic. After a while it got tedious.

The newspapers cartooned him, and the Independent-Republicans invented "Governor Goofy." It stuck and became an instant part of the political folklore. It didn't matter a whole lot that Perpich had the state in good financial condition, that his appointments were uniformly strong, and that the state's reputation as an education innovator earned the esteem of such a nonadmirer of Perpich's as George Bush.

He ran again, unwisely, because he wanted to be vindicated. He ran again because more than any Minnesota politician since Hubert Humphrey, he relished the campaign dust and the rubber chicken marathons. He was a politician vocationally and intuitively. He was better face to face than in the structured environments of press conferences, speeches, and TV, where his ideas often outran his breathless syntax. Folks who talked to him liked him. He was big and hearty, chummy and honest. But the public enthusiasm for Rudy Perpich shriveled in 1990. He started to act remote and quirky. For long stretches he became invisible.

His instincts went wrong in running and wrong in shopping the divorce papers of Jon Grunseth, which he thought revealed the difference between Rudy the family politician and Grunseth. Eventually the swimming pool saga and extramarital sex pushed Grunseth out. It wasn't Perpich who instigated that, but his opponents shrewdly engineered the idea. So to thousands of voters it was Carlson, of all people, who came across as a political white knight to rid the state of both Grunseth the womanizer and Perpich the clown prince. But absent those charges, Grunseth himself would probably have beaten Perpich for the same reason Carlson did. The voters were ready for somebody else.

It means that Rudy's long-running polka dance is over. It was a party. The voters got good government most of the time and a mostly harmless bafflement the rest of the time. Here was Rudy retelling the story of his adolescence as a miner's kid, so enraged by the company's behavior that he picked up a boulder and heaved it through one of the company windows. Here he was campaigning in western Minnesota and being horrified when the program committee put a horse on the same stage to promote a farm show. "Don't do it," Perpich pleaded. "You can't predict what a horse is going to do in public." They should have listened. While Perpich was in full flight of his speech, the horse did his business.

Here was the governor inviting the cream of Minnesota business to one of his private parties in the governor's residence. His wife, the dramatically attractive Lola, was the hostess, moving about sociably like the matriarch at a family reunion on the Range, serving sarma (meat rolls) to the millionaire guests. "You can't believe it," one of the tycoons said later. "It was a fabulous party. It was only time I ever saw the governor and his wife sending the guests home with doggie bags."

For most of his tenure, that was Rudy. He and Lola were the couple who got married on a few bucks while he was still a dentist on the Iron Range. His spartan father sent him on his way from the family house with one piece of luggage, but insisted that the future governor leave the toothbrush because it was family property. He told those stories in flawless Iron Range dialect and had visiting governors and Wall Street barons in hysterics. But when he had to function as the official, Lord-almighty chief executive of Minnesota, he took the role seriously and managed it with urbanity, whether he was toasting Gorbachev or talking to the Norwegian king. He was big and engaging and courtly in the continental manner.

After which he was absolutely convinced the state needed two portraits of Rudy Perpich in the Capitol gallery because he got elected twice.

So in the election the voters were saying, well, it's been fun but adios, Rudy, you had your run. When it was over one could sensibly draw a conclusion. Not many more Rudy Perpiches will happen in state government. That is a reasonably safe guess, and it may be a shame.

In later life Rudy became an international traveler, a kind of town-and-country gentleman, and an exuberant grandfather. But he never really renounced politics, which means you are on shaky ground if you decide to put Rudy Perpich into the political archives. He never did spend much time in the filing cabinets.

unique northerners

Helmer aakvik

At the age of eighty-nine, the old captain's eyes can barely make the horizon. He has closed the crinkled pages of his books of Schopenhauer and Will Durant because he can no longer read.

But he doesn't pretend to be a scholar, so it's not the time, nor in character, for Helmer Aakvik to rail about the indignities of getting old or his approaching blindness.

He can still distinguish the morning sunlight on Lake Superior. It matters if you have been a fisherman for more than sixty years and a seaman whose face and soul were sculpted by the storm.

One of those storms, on Thanksgiving in 1958, turned Aakvik into a national celebrity, if only briefly. For more than thirty hours, he fought off encroaching ice and seas that reached twenty feet to keep his small skiff afloat. Alone in the storm, he tried to rescue another fisherman lost miles from shore and their home village of Hovland, Minnesota.

The ice formed on the gunwales and threatened to sink him. He chipped away at it for hours. He bailed water, hammered at the ice, and drifted in his powerless boat. He did what his brains and his intuition told him. He did it from a lifetime on the water and from what was threaded into his bones by the lore of the Norwegian sea captains when he was a boy in the old country.

When the Coast Guard located him, he was still conscious and capable of handling his boat. He didn't find his friend, Carl Hammer. But he hadn't hesitated in putting out to look for him. Nor had he given up when the night came and the gale rose. Sometimes the sea wins. Yet he never pictured it as an adversary. It is a part of life, something to love on its most benign days and something to contend with during its furies. Although he was never trained in technical seamanship, he knew all about the big water's moods and traps. He learned the cardinal rule early, about holding on to his nerve and good sense when the storms came.

I've never been able to understand why the film producers didn't find him, or discover his extraordinary voyage. In the middle of the supersonic twentieth century, it was one that seemed to define the ancient conflict between man and nature when it rages.

Nobody thought to merchandise his heroism in book or film, least of all the old Norwegian sailor. In the spring he was fishing again. By then parasites and attrition and the markets had signaled the approaching end of commercial fishing for solitary men like Aakvik along the North Shore.

So he has fished for pleasure and for food. He has a gift for being casually thoughtful in things he does and says, and when he speaks it's still in a sure and clear baritone that might have rolled in with the surf. He likes to talk literature, and his wife of fifty-five years, Christine, tells about how he read *The Flying Dutchman* in the Danish language before he left his home in Norway to come to the United States.

I admit a personal bias. I first talked to him on Thanksgiving night in 1958. He had been taken to a hospital in Two Harbors by the Coast Guard and was receiving the prescribed tests and needlework from the flabbergasted attendants. I called from a news association desk in Minneapolis and heard a nursing supervisor explain how impossible it was to talk to the patient. She must have been speaking from his room, because the conversation was interrupted by a bearish Norwegian voice that seemed to rise from the polar fathoms.

"I can speak," he said. He was on the phone without further intervention. Being in an ice storm, he seemed to be telling his nurses, didn't make a sailor an invalid or mute. So we talked. Except for the accent and the latitude, he might have come ashore as Hemingway's Old Man of the Sea, exhausted and grieving over a loss but undefeated and capable of a shrug and a twinkle.

The Old Man of the Sea. It's something old Helmer has had to live with for more than thirty years. The attention he got, and deserved, altered nothing in his life. While he was able, he'd walk down to the lake daily to get water for the kitchen, or split wood for the stove, or caulk his boats. Now and then a news team would visit the spare frame home where he lives with Christine, and there—reconstituted—was that marvelous Scandinavian face, the thick nose, the surging jaw, and the patient and weathered eyes. He fished for auld lang syne until a year or so ago. But the sea lamprey long ago wiped out the commercial trout trade; the herring thinned and so did the ciscoes.

He and Christine met in Clarkfield, Minnesota, where she grew up and where Aakvik came to work as a hired farmhand shortly after he immigrated. They moved to the North Shore a few years later. His urges to roam put their marriage in temporary limbo in the 1950s, when he went to Alaska and she responded with a trip to Norway. They were divorced, but got back together again in Hovland not long afterward to renew their partnership. They never did remarry.

"Maybe you have to be Norwegian to figure that out," a friend said. It clearly caused no anxiety for the partners. About the coming blindness, Aakvik feels no terror. Like the sea, getting old is part of the rhythms of nature.

"I can see," he said. "I can't read anymore, but I can still look out at the lake and I can still cut wood. People ask me about that storm, but I tell you there are things worse. Years later I went out on a June day and the fog came. I have fished off Alaska and in Norway and a lot of other places, but nothing was as bad as this. It was like finding yourself in the middle of a milk bottle. Then the rain came hard, but before that I noticed from a ripple on the water that the weather was coming from the southwest, so I knew about where to head. And I

87

came in almost on top of the place where I wanted. But if I stayed out there a little longer when that rain started to get cold, I wouldn't be here today."

One thing he learned was that a hard life is not the enemy of tenderness. He's retained and deepened that quality. He has taught himself from the great masters of literature, and in his final years he finds himself content to be thankful for that, but still alert to the miracle of sun streamers on the lake.

He has found treasures in being an old man of the sea, without realizing that he himself is one of those treasures.

———————

Helmer Aakvik died in his home on the North Shore in January 1987 at the age of ninety. He was buried in a plain coffin made from the northern woods he loved almost as much as he loved the sea.

Jerry pushcar

It was dangling from the ridgepole of his cabin in the Canadian wilderness, a valentine that looked suspiciously like a two-pound piece of moose meat.

He found it when he returned from a winter day's hunt near Fort Chippewa on Lake Athabasca in northern Alberta. He was 2,000 miles from home, Jerry Pushcar, a quiet, bushwhacking canoeist from Minnesota. He was midway through a three-year odyssey that would carry him 9,000 miles by canoe from New Orleans, Louisiana, to Nome, Alaska.

In the thousands of years in which humans had risked their hides against wild nature for love or fortune, nobody had ever canoed alone from New Orleans to Nome, or seriously considered it. To Jerry Pushcar's knowledge, nobody from Biwabik, Minnesota, had ever received a two-pound moose steak as an invitation to party.

A note was stuck to the cabin door. "Dear Sir," it read. "We came here to visit you but you were not home. We brought you some moose meat. If you like it, you can come and get some more. We are coming to visit you on Wednesday." It was signed "Molly and Marlene."

Pushcar examined his digs glumly. It was the second winter of his journey. He had canoed up the Mississippi River alone from New Orleans to the St. Croix River south of Minneapolis and St. Paul, paddled the St. Croix to northern Wisconsin, and the shoreline of Lake Superior to Grand Portage on the Canadian border. He'd hauled 180 pounds over the historic nine-mile portage of the old voyageurs and then rode the Pigeon and Rainy Rivers to his first winter layover in northwestern Minnesota. From there he canoed the mighty rivers of Canada to Lake Athabasca, and the following year would set out for Nome.

The amateur geographer looks at a map and calls that impossible.

The professional geographer is more clinical. He calls it impossible and too insane to comprehend.

Jerry Pushcar is not a geographer. He is a young man drawn by the wind and stubbornly driven by the idea of facing big nature alone, its glories and its menaces. He didn't get to Athabasca being cowed by problems. So here was another. How was Jerry Pushcar, a somewhat shy bachelor from Minnesota, going to turn himself into a social lion and entertain Molly and Marlene?

His cabin had a certain functional solidity that did credit to the $9.41 it cost to build it. The logs were chinked with moss. Plastic sheet windows kept the gale out, most of the time. His barrel stove kept him warm and fed with fresh game, and only rarely threatened him with asphyxiation.

The visitors delivered on their pledge. They showed up after walking three miles from a tent settlement where they lived with their father, a trapper. The women were a few years younger than Pushcar's twenty-nine years. But they were talkative enough after their host warmly complimented them on their taste in steak. After they taught him a few words of the Cree language, Pushcar reciprocated by singing a few numbers from Minnesota's Iron Range while he played the guitar. Someday, they said, he'd have to teach them that language. One thing led to another until it got to be about 6 P.M., at which time the girls thought it proper to be heading home. He said good-bye and come again. They gave him the equivalent of "Wait a minute, Buster, we thought you were a gentleman. How about walking us home?"

He was a gentleman. He walked them home, more than three miles at twenty-five below zero with a blizzard on the way. His Samoyed, Vagabond, growled his displeasure. The weather wasn't fit for a dog.

But Pushcar got through the blizzard and the winter. He got through Canada. And on May 11, 1977, he trudged a gravel road into Nome, like some north-woods Johnny Appleseed bearing the burrs and aromas of thousands of solitary miles.

Residents gaped, an attitude seldom bestowed on visitors to Nome. People came to this frozen fringe of civilization by plane or boat. They didn't normally canoe 9,000 miles from New Orleans, or walk the last 250 miles over ocean ice and tundra and through three feet of snow.

"We thought you were dead," a bearded house painter told him at the bar of a town saloon. There, the wanderer was toasted with the Nome version of the champagne special: a double boilermaker. Two shots of brandy and a beer.

After that, somebody brought him a Nome newspaper. "I read my own obituary," he said. "I was touched. They said I was lost at sea. I would have sent flowers, but there aren't any flowers on the Alaska tundra two weeks before winter."

His canoe lay cached in a grove of willows along the shore of ice-clogged Norton Sound, a bay of the Bering Sea a few hundred miles south of the Arctic Circle. He ended his unprecedented marathon on foot, hiking over two mountain ranges between the mouth of the Yukon River and Nome.

Purists may complain that technically he didn't canoe the full distance from New Orleans to Nome as he had intended.

Dunk the purists in the Bering Sea. How are you going to execute a J-stroke with a canoe paddle on three feet of ice?

On the last full day of his canoeing, he went for an enforced swim among the ice floes, wearing only his wool underwear. "I pulled in to shore with night coming on and was getting some firewood when I looked up and saw the canoe floating out to sea. I stripped down and swam after it. God, it was cold. I was numb in thirty seconds. The canoe was out about twenty-five to thirty yards, close enough so I could get it before going stiff.

"When I got back, I was shivering so bad I couldn't light a match. I had a little chemical fire-starter. It worked. If it didn't, I think I'd still be back there. I kept thinking about that crazy poem we read in school, about this guy who had a dread of freezing to death on the marge of Lake LaBarge, or something like that. I kept the fire going all day the next day. For six days the wind blew a gale on this little cape where I was stranded. I couldn't put the canoe into the water to try to finish the last 200 miles to Nome. On the seventh day the sun came blasting out of the sky, and it was just a beautiful, calm Alaska morning. I walked down to the shore, looked out on the ocean, and just hauled the canoe back into the bushes and started hiking. There was ice as far as I could see, and there were some seagulls frozen into it."

The libraries swarm with accounts of epic adventure, of the cravings of the human spirit to reach the horizons of the world. There have been longer journeys and more significant ones. But among the explorers of the twentieth century, that little clan of people reaching for something higher or farther or wilder, Jerry Pushcar's deed ranks almost without equal for pure adventure. It needed an authentic passion for the northern night, a gift for understanding loneliness and for being able to sift the out the daily, manageable disasters from the disasters from which there is no return. Pushcar gave it that.

Once in a while you meet a person you suspect has been victimized by some quirky dislocation of stars and genes and wound up in the wrong century. When you study Jerry Pushcar, this becomes more than a suspicion. He was born in northeastern Minnesota in the 1940s and has been trying to prove for years that it was an awful mistake, that it should have been a few hundred years earlier.

This does not seem to be a man of the twentieth century. Hollywood used to do sagas from history about the Jerry Pushcars. They were the deer slayers and the bear fighters of the frontier. They wore buckskin and they went days without eating, sleeping, or washing.

Pushcar long ago denied harboring any heroic qualities—although he does. He calls himself stubborn and inquisitive, a man who is kin to the woods and "maybe a little kinky about wanting to know how far is far."

When he left his canoe in the brush and started hiking through mountains and swamp for Nome, he could afford to reflect. Behind him were three of the mightiest river systems on earth, the Mississippi, the MacKenzie, and the Yukon. He had canoed Lake Superior, the Great Slave Lake, and Athabasca. He had evaded or outnegotiated irritable moose and hostile bears. His first Samoyed dog was poisoned in northern Minnesota, and his second was killed by village dogs at Russian Mission along the Yukon five weeks before he reached the ocean.

After three weeks of walking the tundra, he entered Nome a prepackaged celebrity. Interviewers from the local radio station accompanied him into town. The townspeople found him amiable but something less than a chatterer. It took him a while to put some perspective on his experience of the last three years. Pushcar is woodsy and restrained, all right, but also a man of random spurts of mischievous humor. He is inward but intelligent in the best way for a man of risk and curiosity to be intelligent: He usually makes the right decisions.

So he brings to his adventures (he also canoed 2,000 miles alone from Grand Portage, Minnesota, to Hudson Bay) a mix of the handyman's skills with the child's wonder. "At the start, it was really a case of wanting to know if I could do it," he said after the celebration wore off in Nome. "It was something I set for myself. I didn't have to show anybody else that I had hair on my chest. I really love canoeing alone. Doing it the way I did, well, you have to learn a little more about who you are and a lot more about how much beauty and strength there really is in the wild country, and how good it feels to be part of it. I never had the feeling that I didn't belong there.

"Sometimes, though, I could get to hate the canoe. I had to haul it up fifty miles of rapids through the Richardson Mountains in Canada on the Rat River. With all the fiberglass repairs, and the water that stayed between the layers, the damned thing ended up weighing 125 pounds. But you couldn't really hate the canoe when you were riding free down the Yukon and watching moose graze on the river bank and those mountains rising way off, with snow on the summits.

"Sometimes the loneliness would get to you. But I tried to be constructive. Whenever I got feeling down I did some mental architecture. In my head I built a dream cabin in the woods from the foundation up. Fireplaces in every room, that stuff."

Hundreds met him en route over the years and left their names, thanking him for the stories he told. "I don't think they would have envied the time I nearly got crushed between a barge and the lock gates near Lake Pepin, or the time the wild dogs almost chewed me up in Arkansas, or that mother eagle north of Winnipeg.

"I saw this eagle's nest high in a tree and scrambled up to take a picture. I'm a freak about pictures. I didn't molest the baby eagle. I wouldn't harm something like that for the world. But I couldn't convince the mother eagle. I heard a terrific screech and turned just in time to avoid this huge swooping bird. It nearly took my head off. I disappeared fast."

His memories, though, probably won't pay the rent, and he plans to do some carpentering in Nome before deciding what to do with the rest of his life—which probably has room in it someplace for a canoe.

The thought of feminine company after all those years in the bush is not entirely foreign to the young bachelor. "I almost had a romance with one of those young woman who brought the moose steak at Athabasca. After a couple of weeks I moved down to the trappers' settlement to get better acquainted. I'd like to write to that place, but I don't think they pick up mail more than once a year. It's not the best arrangement for a steady romance. I am interested though, in meeting a woman who likes the woods the way I do."

The man does leave you with a thought. One way or another, he'll manage.

———————

After years of roaming, Jerry Pushcar returned to St. Paul and met a lovely young woman named Marilyn Dettinger. After their marriage, they settled in Nome, where the wanderer mixed his wilderness urges with the domestic pursuits of being a husband, father, and carpenter. For months at a time, he and Marilyn and later the kids would go up into the bush near Nome and mine or pan for gold. Pushcar was better at adventuring than most and better at mining than practically any prospector of the post-Klondike. He took away several thousand dollars in gold dust in each exploration and then dutifully walked away from it each time to resume family life in Nome. Marilyn died in the winter of 1995 of an illness unrelated to their rugged life. Devastated by the loss, Jerry considered not returning to Alaska with his sons, now thirteen and ten. In the end, they went back and are now living again in Nome. He still builds, and will again roam the wilderness when the time is right.

Dinna madsen

Her snowshoes were soggy with slush. Every fifteen or twenty steps she would stop to remove it. She was tired but careful. She cleaned her snowshoes methodically and lovingly, because while she was doing it she felt movement inside her.

Snowshoeing across a frozen lake wouldn't have been hard for her at another time, when she was trim and nimble. But on this day she was walking across the ice of Lake Saganaga toward a hospital.

In January of 1956 in Minnesota, women were battling city traffic to take the kid to an ice arena. Others were hauling the kid to ballet lessons. Dinna Madsen was snowshoeing across a north-woods lake to have a baby.

Her midwinter journey with an unborn child by dogsled and on snowshoes remains today one of those wilderness epics that never quite ends.

Why should it? The child who was born a week later is now thirty-five, a mother of two living in Tacoma, Washington. Dinna's husband is eighty-six, an Englishman who went to North America to trap in the Canadian woods and is still robust, although at the moment he's sunning himself in New Zealand with relatives.

And Dinna Madsen is now seventy but irreversibly Dinna. No one else need apply. On Friday, in the soft air of a autumn day at the lakeside resort on Saganaga, she made out a grocery list for the boat trip and sixty-mile drive down the Gunflint Trail to Grand Marais. She was in good voice. She's almost always in good disposition. So she reminisced.

"Six miles across that lake," she said. "It's a piece of cake in September. It wasn't like that in January of 1956. That was an adventure, that's for sure."

The sparse and windburned clan of lake dwellers on the Minnesota-Canada border is made of individualists. Dinna may be a little more individual than most. She and her life link the wilderness frontier with the space age. She doesn't sound historic. She is saucy and jubilant. She is talkative and more or less imperishable.

She is Dinna.

In January of 1956 she was going to give birth in about a week. It was the kind of winter to send the wolves to Florida. It already had piled up more than 100 inches of snow and a stretch of cold weather in which the cabin squatters would cheer when the temperature got above twenty below zero. Art Madsen got squirmy about Dinna's due date. "You ought to go to Duluth early to give yourself some leeway in case the roads are bad," he said.

After Art ferried his wife to the mainland, he was going to stay at their island resort with two of their small children. Chris, six, was going to Duluth with Dinna. While Art worked to get his snow machine ready to take his wife across the lake and on an eventual ride to the North Shore via the Gunflint road, an ice fisherman they both knew came by with his propeller-driven snowboat. They put Dinna and Chris aboard.

"I was wearing everything I could," Dinna said. "That snowboat didn't have enough fuel to get us all the way to the landing. So we got off. Another fellow was going to pick us up in his machine, but when he came by he was loaded with furs and I said, 'It's all right, I'll wait for Art, my husband.'"

She didn't know that Art couldn't get his machine going. She and the boy were in the channel not far from Seagull River. The temperature was below zero. The boy looked at his mother. He had come to believe there wasn't much she couldn't do to take care of her family in a remote world where common sense is almost as important as love. But he had to ask a question. "Think we can start a fire?"

The situation seemed to preclude any elaborate rhetoric. She said, "Sure."

They gathered sticks and birch bark and tore up an old tree stump to start it. She did it with one match. They stood over the flames getting warm for a while and then saw Art pulling a toboggan across the ice and starting to fume as he got closer. "The last thing he wanted to see was Chris and me standing out there in the open air. He threw his mitts down and asked why in hell didn't I go in on one of those machines. I told him what happened, and he told me what happened to his machine. He had some snowshoes with him. He gave them to me and put my suitcase on the toboggan because we still had three miles to go to get to the landing, where I could get a ride. Art and the boy walked in their boots. It was cold but there was slush on the lake, so it was hard going."

But it was the beginning. Several days later, Ade Toftey of the *Cook County News-Herald* sat down and wrote it as carefully and briefly as he could. This was the north woods. You don't talk much about heroics. Things more or less tell themselves. He called the Associated Press office in Minneapolis. I remember Ade because I was in the office at the time. We took his story, without moving a comma, and put it on the international wire:

"She left her small children at the cabin with her husband. She went by dog team down Saganaga Lake to the Jock Richardson place . . ."

People read it in Paris. Dinna knows, because she got mail from Paris three or four months after it was written. In those days, nobody faxed. And nobody operated a medical clinic on the end of the Gunflint Trail.

"The baby kept moving," she said. "Art was afraid we were going to have it right there. I started going through the checklist. You know how it is. Take it easy but push. Hurry up but go slow."

Dinna.

"The road didn't come all the way to the lake. One of the fishermen had a dog team, and they put me on the sled. Art had to go back to our island. We went for a mile or so with the dog team until we came across George Plummer and Charlie Cook waiting for the mail. It was getting colder all the time, and finally Georgie said they should take Chris and me to Russell Blankenburg's resort and wait for the snowplow there. He was able to get his car through there, and we spent the night in a cabin at Russell and Eve Blankenburg's. They had a little wood heater in there and there must have been seven sleeping bags on me, but when the fire went out I found my boots frozen to the floor.

"The Blankenburgs called the county snowplow custodian and wanted to know when the plow was coming. He was gloomy. They counted seventeen inches of new snow. The road was closed for twelve miles. It was hard to see how they could get through.

"Mrs. Blankenburg told the man, 'Listen. My husband is the biggest taxpayer in the county, and we've got an expectant mother here, and we want to see that snowplow.' "

They saw the snowplow.

So Dinna and Chris got a ride down the Gunflint into Grand Marais and took a bus down the North Shore to Duluth, where a few days later at St. Luke's Hospital, Helen Sue, forever afterward known as Suzie, arrived safely and warmly.

She and her family visit the wild country as often as they can, which means periodic reunions at Sagonta, the Madsen home and resort on the island. It has been their sanctuary and their business for more than fifty years, dating to the time when a teenage milk deliverer from Duluth named Dinna took her mother's advice and "went out in the world." It was a trip that took her roughly 150 miles up the North Shore, through the Gunflint, and to the resorts at the end of the civilized world as it existed in northern Minnesota in the 1940s. She met the Englishman, and they have lived the life both of them idealized.

Romantic? Sure. Painful? Sure. Of their six children, Chris was killed in an accident not long after he came back from Vietnam, and Chuckie fell from the dock and drowned when he was 3. Much of the wilderness disappeared, but the lakes still glisten in the summer, and birds feed from their hands. The blizzard screams outside the cabin in winter, but when it abates Dinna takes her snowshoes or skis or boots and goes for a hike.

"It's never as beautiful as it is in the middle of winter. But, hey, those kids of Suzie's. They're great at the piano and ice skating and you ought to seem them on unicycles when they come to Grand Marais . . ."

Dinna. She slogged through snow for miles to have a baby, but you can't tell her today from any grandma in the world until the blizzard comes.

And then she is different.

Dorothy molter

The sun's daily career is short and wistful in early winter along the Minnesota-Canada border.

At 4:30 P.M. it disappears and leaves the wilderness to the wind and stars, and now to the echoes and memory of Dorothy Molter, trudging across the ice to her cabin, alone but not lonely.

I met her only a few times. Our talk was cordial. It was the kind of talk that never threatened the borders of profundity, although it was almost hypnotic for me. And one winter at Christmas time I spent the night alone in the Boundary Waters woods, bundled in my sleeping bag and tent. Once in a while in those years I skied into the winter woods alone for a few days, when I wouldn't hear another human voice or see another face. It was a way to meet nature in its purest, wildest form. Yet it was also unnatural, because humans need other humans, and a few solitary days in winter are a retreat rather then any serious plunge into hermitage. But on that night I thought about Dorothy Molter. And it occurred to me that each year at Christmas time we slip into a few moments of harmless reverie, trying to visualize a world in which the harmonies and simple humilities of a Christmas night could last the year round.

Dorothy Molter, I said. There was at least one person I knew who must feel something close to a Christmas peace from one season into another, who knew how to preserve its mellow song each day of her life.

That small longing the rest of us feel lasts only a few hours before it gets pretty well ground up by reality. People fight, bills arrive, and the telephone goes nuts. The way we do Christmas now, if it lasted

365 days we would be standing in the registration line to a mental asylum. But we know in our hearts that those few hours of shared gentleness and magnanimity in the world are worth it, and for that reason there's nothing wrong with imagining a life where there is true internal calm. Such a life doesn't have to be a saint's. It can be a Dorothy Molter's.

I may have evoked Dorothy's memory that night in the Boundary Waters because there were Christmas nights in her life when she sat staring at the aurora borealis, alone on her island in the pines, suffused by the glory of it.

Dorothy was a person of ordinary virtues who created an extraordinary life by discovering herself, being content with what she found, and understanding both her horizons and her limits. Relationships were good, but she did not have to be dependent on them. There are some kinds of love that do not require passion, some kinds of peace that do not need evangelism.

In the few times I talked to her, she struck me as a person who seldom looked for any dramatic definition or symbolism in her solitary life in the north woods. She was civil and pleasant as a conversationalist, never pretending that she was some kind of reborn Bird Woman facing a frontier. As the mistress of her little island in the Boundary Waters for fifty-six years, she was a collector and a putterer. She grew things and collected recipes, ornaments, letters, and the names of thousands of canoeists who dropped in to chat. She lived isolated for months, but she was not a recluse. Her limits were her fundamental needs: a kinship with the earth, her understanding of her place in it, and an appreciation of both the earth and the people who passed through her life.

Her life on her island was not an escape. It was a union of her spirit with the winds of autumn, the wolf's call at night, the solemnities of winter, and the eagerness of spring. She had a kind of stolid physique that cloaked her femininity. She had a psychological toughness and stubbornness that did not conflict with the poetry she felt when the sun burst over the lake and renewed her.

She read her books and wrote her letters, and once in a while she strapped on her snowshoes and trudged for hours on the frozen lakes to reach the town of Ely. Sometimes she would be awakened by a wolves' chorale on the ice a few hundred feet from her cabin. When snowmobiles came, it was easier to keep her pantry stocked and more fun, too, because she genuinely enjoyed the yarn telling and the small talk. But when the visitors were gone, she became the custodian of her island again, tuned to the sounds of the lake and forest. "One of the sounds I've always liked best is the water in summer," she said one night when we stopped to say hello in midwinter. "We don't have huge waves here. But you can go down to the water when the sun has been up for an hour or so and things are warm, and birds are calling and feeding, and the water along the shore just seems to be telling you that the world is OK, and you don't need much more than this."

The world might not allow many more Dorothy Molters. But what she was saying was that if you bring to the world limits you can understand and appreciate, peace might follow. She found it on an island. The rest of us may not be so venturesome or lucky, but she'd say it's there if you look.

Her admirers were never sure how to classify her, whether she was a frontier woman or a north woods Florence Nightingale. You get the impression that if the Canadian jays at her suet board could talk, they would address the lady with the braids as "your highness."

They could do that fondly despite her big and knotted woodchopper's hands that cut cords of firewood, fired rifles at marauding bears, and mended the wounds of passing canoeists. They stopped at her island in the summer to drink her homemade root beer and to snack on her dream bars and tell her how much they envied her life on the island. Her nod was her graceful acknowledgment. She didn't bring up the squabbling she had to do with the bureaucrats or the fright she felt in winter storms in the early years. She was a nurse when she was young. She had tried both the city and the woods. In the mid-1930s she decided she could live without the debatable gifts of city speed and turmoil. She moved to her three tiny islands on Knife Lake, a quarter of a mile from the lake's American shore.

Before the snowmobile, she was the only stir of humanity throughout the long white winter from Otter Track Lake to the Moose Lake Landing, fifteen miles to the southwest. She'd snowshoe to the landing two or three times each winter to drop off or pick up mail and replenish her supplies. She'd go for her morning hikes into the frozen bay to check her water hole in the ice or to exercise in her snowshoes. In later years a snowmobile motor would intrude on the stillness. It never offended her. She owned one herself. Living alone in the woods doesn't mean a person isn't sociable. Among the snowmobile clubbers of Ely, Babbitt, and Winton, it was de rigueur to stop at Dorothy's island and unreel the latest jack-pine gossip. This Dorothy liberally fueled with her cookies and endless cascades of coffee.

I last talked to her in the 1970s, after camping on the shore in December. Approaching her cabin, you could see the lantern in the window casting amber shafts through the porch screens. Her three islands were connected with minibridges. During some summers she lived in a tent and from her little commissary sold her root beer by the hundreds of bottles to passing canoeists. But that was summer.

In December, she welcomed me to the warmth of her stove, her house, and her table. She was then sixty-five, a woman with an open, fleshy face. Her smile was restrained and pensive, but what it really pictured was her modesty and calm. She was a large woman with the owl's fondness for constructive activity at night. Her routine was to stay up until three or four in the morning, sitting at her dining table, writing letters to the hundreds of old acquaintances and canoeists she met in the summer. Many of them wrote four and five times. She answered all, and later she'd compile some of the correspondence in a booklet.

Her cabin in December was a jolly clutter of Christmas decorations, goodies, and mementoes left by friends. She had bought pendants and ornaments on which she laced intricate geometric designs of angels' hair. Her refrigerator was the natural ice. Her light came from the two white sacs on her Coleman burners. She'd lived through blizzards, guided fishermen and hunters in the prime of her life, and slogged through waist-high drifts. She shoveled and chopped, but she was every ounce a feminine.

"I think what I like best about living alone up here is the quiet," she said. "I also like the different attitudes you get from the change in season. The spring is best. The woods come alive again. The summer is busy and beautiful. The fall makes you think and the winters make you struggle a little. But to see the flowers and the birds and leaves again, that makes it all worth it.

"I do love it. Sometimes people ask if this is a life for a woman. I have to say, why not a woman?"

She was the daughter of an itinerant railroad man who introduced her to the Minnesota's north woods nearly sixty years ago. As a trained nurse, she gave care to a retired logger who owned the islands then. When he died, he bequeathed her the islands and cabins. She made an annual trip to Chicago for years to renew her nurse's license, but in time settled in to become, with the death of Bennie Ambrose a few lakes over, the last year-round inhabitant of the Boundary Waters canoe country. Federal law threatened to evict them in the mid-1970s. But the government yielded to the cries of their friends and admirers, and to common sense. The government said they could stay as long as they lived, which they did.

Outside her window that December, the jays and chickadees yakked around the bird feeder with its suet and assorted groceries. Dorothy shared a confidence. "Right now, I'm dieting. One meal a day for Dorothy." She wasn't so sure about the wolves. "I saw the strangest thing not long ago," she said. "I heard something about ten in the morning and went outside the porch. There they were, lined up together, right near my water hole, twelve wolves. They were doing a little yelping but not much. I don't think I was scared. They didn't seem too interested in me. I went back into the cabin for a minute, and when I came out they were walking slowly across the lake, single file."

And Dorothy watched them go, holding not a rifle but a camera.

She died at seventy-nine in her log cabin in December 1986. It was a few days before a Christmas she would have observed with her angels' hair and her search of the sky for the aurora borealis, which always told her this was the northern night, and all in the world was well.

There's a simple memorial to Dorothy Molter, the revered matriarch of the wild country, on her island in the pines in the Boundary Waters of northern Minnesota. It is a country in which, for so many years, she was a breath and a heartbeat of civility.

Jerri kyle

On some mornings, the sun rising over Lake Superior bursts into the windowed porch where Jerri Kyle sleeps, and the swish of the surf against the rocks turns time around.

For many years she needed no other geography in her life. There was the great water and the orange globe leaping out of it to spread its warmth. This and Jerri Kyle. Nothing more. She'd awake, toss off the covers, and wriggle and grunt into her wheelchair to get the coffee going in the kitchen.

The world now being in order, she'd trundle back into her porch. It had inexplicable powers to transform time. She was sure of that. At some hours this place was her Oz. Freaky figures arrayed themselves outside her window, sculpted by the sea spray in winter or by the wind savaging the tree limbs in the fall.

Other nights it was her sanctuary, not from the rudeness of the world but from her temptations to be soured by it.

Her Tinkertoy cabin by the lake was never an escape. She didn't need flight. What she needed were the cries of the gulls. She needed the sun's rays drying out the ancient red slab rock that had been laundered for centuries by the lake. When the sun did that, the earth and Jerri Kyle were cleansed.

Although it seemed to shift identities on a whim, her porch reverted to a workaday role about 9 A.M. each day. It was her studio. One day she'd paint a gull landing on a roosting rock in the bay. The next day she might write a poem about the unlimited dreams of a turtle.

After this summer, her Oz will be gone.

More correctly, it will belong to somebody else. After six years she is selling her North Shore cottage to take an apartment overlooking a suburban shopping center outside of Duluth, a place not famous for transforming time.

An old friend visiting her asked why. How could she abandon the spray of the big breakers and the squawking gulls for a suburban apartment? Was it money, loneliness, what? If it was money, why not sell the old cement mixer she'd squirreled away?

"It's none of that," she said. "The winters never get lonely, but they do get to be a hassle for one person trying to keep up the place." She didn't say one woman, or one disabled woman struck by polio when she was ten.

She made her acceptances years ago, first when she lost the use of her legs, and later when she lost her marriage through divorce not long after she and her husband moved into the cottage a few miles north of Two Harbors.

Some time before that she found out she could paint well enough to sell. After a few more years she made the same discovery about poetry, which may be harder to sell than old plastic. She writes about the sunrise and fields of flax and about dreams and foolishness. Pretty standard fare. But she has a feel for reverie without drenching it in emotionalism.

Conversationally, she giggles and spews out putdowns of her labors and her solitary life. But the visitor never has trouble figuring out that this is harmless posturing, her way of being social. She doesn't want to make something profound out of living alone by the big lake in the north woods. She does the same with her spiritual life, which is a mixture of conventional religion with random plunges into psychic power.

She doesn't call it spiritualism. But from the time her mother died she found herself treading on the edges of a spirit world. She is convinced there are times when she is being guided to draw this or to write that. Whatever is moving her does it expertly. She idealizes nature and human relationships, searching for tenderness in how we treat nature, how nature treats us, and how we treat each other. Privately, she sometimes spoofs the intensity of that search. Jerri and her muse. She laughs often, and it enhances the attractiveness of her strong and animated face. She does it in trills and arpeggios, as though trying to find music in the delight she feels at the moment. She experienced that often in her first years of solitude by the lake. Winter was a gift of God rather than a penance for life in Minnesota. The frozen water pipes and high snowdrifts she had to deal with were somewhat less impressive gifts. She pretended to grumble about those and about her predicaments getting in and out of the wheelchair. But she was amazingly adroit at it.

Finally, though, she decided that was taking her into the life of a recluse. She enjoys human chatter too much for that. She likes to talk poetry and art with other members of a tiny arts society that gives her energy.

Now she's a suburban woman. The groceries are easier to fetch. There are more voices to mix with, and long talks about free verse lubricated with a few cans of beer. Then, as before, her disability seems rarely to absorb her. She calls September the season of her soul, and in September I bought a little sketch she drew of Split Rock Lighthouse encircled by gulls. It was done with grace and insight and must be worth five times what I paid for it. Since we've been friends for years, she refused to take more.

Of the sketch she wrote, "I will wait my appointment each September until another moment when I, too, perhaps shall appear in a new time, in another season . . . to love again."

———————

Life in the winter for a disabled woman, even one with the will and the creativity of Jerri Kyle, can become burdensome. Jerri sold her cottage by the lake in the late 1970s and moved to an apartment in suburban Duluth high on the headland above Lake Superior. She wrote and sketched there with as much zeal as before, and died a few years later, not far from the lake.

one day at a time

Bell ringer

He was one of those Christmas bell ringers, a nondescript sort of guy in his later years. His wrinkled face was pinched a little tighter by the winter breeze, and sometimes he would put his free hand in his pocket to get it warm.

His station was one of the entrances in Southdale. His harvest was mixed. The contributions looked about normal, a dollar here and there, clinking coins, and once in a while a bill with Abe Lincoln in the center oval.

A passerby would guess that he had done this before, maybe for years. His wrist stroke looked practiced and economical, and he tried to be sociable with some of the shoppers, although the standing and the bell ringing appeared to tire him.

He was just one more Salvation Army bell ringer, one of the anonymous people bluntly installed at the scene of society's bounty to squeeze our consciences.

But if you looked more closely, there was a difference. He wasn't adequately dressed for his chores. While the cold was not severe, his workaday jacket seemed skimpy. It was open at the collar, and the inexpensive shirt needed another layer.

The man ringing his bell for gifts to the neglected and lonely looked just as lonely himself.

The Salvation Army colonels don't organize high-velocity sales seminars for the bell ringers. You will see a charismatic bell ringer, but not very often. They don't look or feel noble. Soliciting for poor people is a job some people need, the way Santa Clausing is a job.

Ring-a-ling. That's what they do. Showmanship isn't part of the deal. The one-liners belong to the Santa Clauses inside.

But once in a while the bell ringer becomes something more.

He is Christmas because he is standing there in a cheap jacket while hundreds of people rush by into the palaces of glass, fur, and baubles.

He is the contradiction of Christmas: We know we have to play the game, spending money in those palaces, but we also know that if there is a grace to this time of the year, it is in the sound of that cold and lonely man's bell, summoning us to rediscover a better part of what we have learned about living, and about our humanity.

He is Christmas because he seemed to be as much a pilgrim as a conscience. He was surrounded by affluence, which he did not resent, and he stood doggedly ringing his bell, wearing a scruffy jacket in the advent of what is called a time of glory.

A woman approached him as he shivered. She was well dressed, friendly, and straightforward. She was carrying something in a bag.

"I thought about you when I was shopping," she said. "You do your job well, and you're a nice man. I wanted you to know."

She handed him a thin box. He opened it and found a new scarf.

He seemed startled. He recovered, smiled, and thanked her. He said he thought it was wonderful. And then she handed him her second gift, a pair of insulated gloves.

He asked her name. She said she was Elizabeth. He took the gloves and clasped them, gave her his name, and said he would never have expected a stranger to do this for him.

They spoke for a few more moments and said good-bye.

There is scant chance they will ever see each other again. But what they gained from each other for a few minutes at a bell ringer's stand in a shopping center will be an imperishable part of their Christmas observance for the rest of their lives.

And it reminded the witness that there is nothing magical about it. It is available to all.

Carole page

When they were playing in the Hopkins High School band in the 1960s, she brought him flowers on impulse. Sometimes they were wildflowers, sometimes daisies plucked from the neighbor's yard. They were in love and her flowers colored their day.

Their lives took different directions the next year, and their romance ended. But fourteen years later, as a wife and mother living in Oregon, she brought him flowers again and placed them on Rick Ewald's grave at Fort Snelling.

This time they colored her clinging sense of loss.

She talked to him as though he were there. She talked about things deep and things that were nutty. But for years after the graveyard visit, she was afraid she had left some of her emotions unspoken.

So in 1985 on a drizzling day in Washington, D.C., Carole Wedding Page stood before the black granite wall of the Vietnam Veterans Memorial and placed an envelope beneath a panel on which the name of Richard Clayton Ewald was etched.

The letter she left was a schoolgirl's song of affection and trust, enriched by a mature woman's recognition of what the death of one decent young man on a Vietnam battlefield two decades ago had meant to the world, but mostly to her.

It was intended to be a letter to Rick Ewald, tuba player, soldier, and what his mother called "a dreamer." Today, the letter has become part of the nation's reconciliation with itself, its words read by hundreds of thousands. They are respectful, gentle, and intimate words. There are words that rekindle the breeziness of their adolescent days, and others that seem to rise not only from Carole Page's soul but out of the nation's conscience.

"It was important for me to come today . . . to touch your name on the wall that makes it all real . . . I'm still trying to say good-bye. I never managed that very well with us, did I? But you made all of that OK and that made a big difference in my life."

He was a young man, twenty-one, who had wept the night before leaving for Vietnam, not wanting to go. But he became a good and sacrificing soldier, who was killed when he stood to give covering fire for the men of his squad.

The mingled cry of bereavement and thanksgiving in Carole Page's letter appears in a recently published book by Random House, *Shrapnel in the Heart*, by Laura Palmer. It brings together the farewells of wives, children, parents, friends, and comrades to some of the 52,132 Americans who died in the war that millions of other Americans hated and derided. The letters were left at the memorial wall with scraps of poems and mementos, later collected by the National Park Service. Together they form a spontaneous testament and hymn from voices long unheard: the loved ones of those who died in the unloved war.

Those letters might be read to express the nation's contrition. Much of the country forgot that good people fight and die in bad wars. And the country therefore created its own frigid no-man's-land to which Vietnam veterans came back, unhonored.

The letters weren't meant to say that, but they do. For that reason they matter to America today.

"When I left my letter for Rick at the wall," Carol said in Eugene, Oregon, "I felt that I had finally been able to say good-bye to a friend who should never have left us. I had not come to a closure with my emotions as they were affected by Rick's life and death. He and the man I married were the only men with whom I've ever been in love. We didn't exchange letters after he left for Vietnam. He didn't send his address.

"We loved each other in high school, and it was wonderful. We played miniature golf together someplace on Highway 7. We'd go out to Lincoln Del or Bernie's in St. Louis Park, and we had a hundred laughs playing in band together. He was a skinny kid with disorderly straw hair, and he played a tuba. I played the drums. I had just moved to Hopkins with my family from Redwood Falls. He was a year ahead of me. He had good things to say about everybody, and he was always thoughtful and funny, and I started looking forward to seeing him every morning. I began picking flowers to give him, and when I wrote notes to him I pressed a flower with them.

"He left for St. Cloud State in the fall of 1966. I had to write to him in his freshman year to tell him my feelings had changed, and I would have to return his class ring. I asked if our friendship could continue."

She knew he had a right to be resentful. But he accepted. He didn't argue or campaign to change her mind. The next time he wrote, he wrote in friendship. She respected him immensely for that. But he always began his notes with "Hi, lover," a slangier and less literal form of the word than it is today.

And that is how she began the letter she left at the wall.

"I remember being in my parents' home in Hopkins one day late in 1968. Dick Page, whom I met at St. Olaf and who is now my husband, was there with me to study. My mother came in with a copy of the *Minneapolis Star*. It used to print pictures of the local boys who died in Vietnam. She was standing there silently crying and looking down at the newspaper. Rick's picture was there. It was awful. That marvelous kid was gone, and it was even worse knowing I'd lost touch with him the last six months of his life."

She cried in her room at college the day of his funeral but didn't attend. She wasn't sure whether her presence would have been an intrusion on his family, and she wasn't sure of his mother's feelings toward her. It was an anxiety that Eleanor Ewald says today was misplaced, and she feels nothing but goodwill toward the woman who wrote so honestly to and of her son.

"Rick kept a lot of stuff inside of him," his mother said in her St. Louis Park home. "He thought about everybody except himself. He should have been a good student but he did a lot of dreaming. His grades weren't great at St. Cloud. He left there and went to night school at the university, but he came home one day and said he couldn't concentrate because he was going into the Army. He didn't really want to go, but he never thought of trying to get out of it. He wrote once about getting nicked by shrapnel, and the medical officer said he was putting him in for the Purple Heart. 'Mom,' he said, 'you can cut yourself with a knife here and they'd put you in for the Purple Heart.'"

Don't call Rick Ewald brave, he was saying.

But we will.

He didn't want to lead the squad into combat when the squad leader was called out, but he did. He didn't want to be a soldier in Vietnam. But when the gunfire came on the day he fell, he was a soldier protecting those around him. The United States of America awarded the Silver Star and Bronze Star to the boy who once played tuba in the Hopkins High School band and got flowers from Carole Ann Wedding.

With her dentist husband, Dr. Dick Page, and their two children, she moved to Eugene, Oregon, in the 1970s. Visiting the Twin Cities in 1979, she took some flowers to Ewald's grave and sat beside the white marker. It is a few hundred yards from where his father, Robert, a Marine veteran of the Tinian, Saipan, and Tarawa battles of World War II, is buried. "My husband understood the need for me to complete my good-byes," she said.

"Later, after Laura Palmer called me about including my letter in her book, I had doubts. I felt vulnerable and uncertain about it. When the memorial wall replica came to Eugene, I went every night, watching others experiencing the wall, and lit candles to warm a friend's visit to my rainy city. I silently debated with myself about whether sharing Rick's life and a part of mine could be healing for others. When I decided the answer was yes, I wrote another note to Rick to tell him that I was scared, that I wished he had just come home, that maybe the book would help. Then I said good-bye again."

The next night when she visited the wall in Eugene she found an unsigned note addressed to Carole, written on paper made in Minnesota.

"Dear Carole,

"I did come home in the hearts and minds of each of the living. Every man and woman that came back brought a part of me. I have talked to you with their voices and loved you with their hearts. Don't be scared for I am always with you. I will always be there in the still of the night. Be still, listen, you will hear my voice."

She didn't recognize the handwriting, and she doesn't assign it to the supernatural. It was from a friend speaking a truth. And the truth is that the ones who died in Vietnam are no longer without a voice.

October, 1985

Hi Lover:

Seventeen years . . . you're still twenty-one—forever young, but gone. Murdered. And nothing will make your loss to us less of a tragedy.

The first gray hairs sneak onto my head as I face thirty-seven. I look into the eyes of my teenage son and I wonder—have we done enough to change things . . . have we done enough . . .

Waddaya say, kid—I brought you flowers. I always brought you flowers, didn't I? Picked from the neighbors' yards on the way to the school bus . . . It's how we fell in love. And then I gave you daisies in the midst of all those white slabs of death.

Your slab said they gave you a purple heart—for dying. Well, this here letter is a purple heart for living. I thought it might mean more to you. The paper is a gift from my daughter—she

119

loves purple. She's 10 and 3/4 years old and beautiful, and someday she'll have a first love too. I hope he has your kindness and humor. And when she's thirty-seven and still looking for some of those answers, I hope they can touch one another and talk of how they've changed and say thanks for having been a part of my life when everything still lay ahead.

It was important for me to come today . . . to touch your name on the wall that makes it all real . . . I'm still trying to say good-bye. I never managed that very well with us, did I? But you made all of that OK and that made a big difference in my life. The only way I've ever known to pay you back for that gift is to live my life as if it mattered and to work every day in every way for what is right.

Oh, it was wonderful to be in love in the Spring of '65. That part of you will always be alive—love doesn't divide, it multiplies. And the me I bring to the wonderful life and love I share with Dick and our precious, precious children is a me that is a part of you.

I'll always bring you flowers. You gave me love. Good-bye. Hello.

Carole Ann

Hoa larson

Police bullets tore into the walls and war ruins in Vietnam a few feet from him as he ran to the waterfront. He heard cries.

Some of the escaping youngsters fell dead. He didn't know it then. He kept racing for a boat that would take him to the unknown sanctuary in the ocean, and then to America. He was a nine-year-old boy, a victim of the war in which his father was killed.

On his birth registries in Vietnam he was called Pham The Hoa (Pham-Tay-Wah).

On the court of Williams Arena in the Minnesota boys state high school basketball tournament this week, ten years after his escape, he will line up for Fergus Falls against Bloomington Jefferson as Hoa Larson, point guard. And in the footnotes of the years of trauma and slaughter of the war in Vietnam and its aftermath, he comes as a witness. He is a witness first to his mother's bravery, and then to the embrace of another family and another people, in western Minnesota thousands of miles from the house where his mother said good-bye to her two sons.

She said they would meet again. And a few days ago he discovered that they will, possibly this year.

Expect jitters from this kid for a few minutes at Williams Arena. They are mandatory. Nobody plays in a state basketball tournament without them. But expect no terror in the eyes of this point guard, eighteen.

He has heard worse sounds than thousands of screeching voices. He heard the rifle shots overhead, the moans of the dying, and the threats of government guards in the jail where he, his mother, and his brother were held after two failed escape attempts from Ho Chi Minh City—called Saigon until 1975. He heard the hopeless curses and anguish of the refugee boat's captain, after the seaman's brother fell overboard in heavy seas and they could not turn back to look for him.

He heard the sounds of a baby born in the escaping boat a few hours after they put out to sea in darkness.

"The 105 people in the boat slept on top of each other, it was so crowded for the three days it took us to get to a camp on an island in Malaysia," he said. "We lived there for six months. My mother couldn't leave Saigon. She said we would have a better chance without her. She said some day we would find our way to America. And now, so will she."

But expect no solemn poses from Hoa Larson today. This is a focused, confident, and sunny kid whose brown eyes snap with the daily amazements of life as a high school student and member of the family in Fergus Falls, Minnesota. Is he a refugee? Yes, that. He came here so designated in the early 1980s through Lutheran Social Services to join the family of Katheryn and Larry Larson, a Trans-World pilot, as a foster child. Is he motivated? Yes, that too. The senior class at Fergus Falls runs to more than 200 students. Hoa Larson is number four, with a grade point average of 3.96. Would you guess mathematics and science, technology? Sure. It buzzes creatively in his head. But is he also a closet reformer?

"When he first started evaluating American food," Katheryn Larson said, "he thought it was good but bland by Oriental standards. So we started using sauces. Today in this house, we put Tabasco on EVERYTHING. He didn't insist. It's just an accommodation. East meets West."

Pham The Hoa meets Fergus Falls.

"When I first got to Fergus Falls with my brother, who is two years older, I liked it like I do now but I couldn't figure out where all the people were," Hoa said. "Saigon was life on the streets. There were people everywhere. Crowded, crowded. My mother had a house, but you sort of lived where you were on the street. When I came to Fergus Falls it took me a little while to figure out that there weren't as many people there as in Saigon. But I thought everybody in Fergus Falls ought to be walking around in the street."

Somebody then told him about the settled life of the prairie. And he settled. The Larson family made it easy. With three grade-school kids of their own, they spread the manageable chaos to include Hoa and his brother, Phong. The early tensions disappeared fast. The love in the expanded family was general and often noisy.

Hoa learned American English in swift gulps, as he learns almost everything. He began to learn English partly by tying it in with the strategy of chess, which he plays often but not with the exuberance of his basketball. He will play that way in the tournament. But first, sometime between the coach's last counsel and the tip-off, he will remember another world.

"My father was a lieutenant in the South Vietnamese Army. He was killed in combat when I was two. When the war was over and the Americans left, my mother worried about my brother and me being drafted into their army. She saved her money. She worked as a weaver, and she worked all the time. The only way you could buy passage on one of the refugee boats was with gold. She got it. The first two times we failed and were jailed. The third time she said to us, 'If they catch you again, you have a better chance of getting out than if I'm with you. Go. If you get to America, work hard and make something of yourselves. I will always think of you."

The Larsons, grieving over the death of a fourth child shortly after birth, were moved to bring a Vietnamese into their family. They saw films taken in the island refugee camp. The footage included pictures of Hoa and Phong. In time, they arrived, brought to Fergus Falls in part by the First Lutheran Church congregation.

"We were scared to death on all sides when we first met," she said.

"But the fact that we had kids their age helped immeasurably. Our neighbors and friends, hundreds of townspeople, and the kids at school joined. Phong is now a student at North Dakota State. Hoa? He's energy and intelligence and friendship. He's also impulsive and one of us. We're 'Mom and Dad' to him. He's an assertive kid. He's challenging and learning all the time, but nobody is threatened by his manner because it's up-front and the goodwill in him is obvious. He'll probably go on to Minnesota-Morris, which is a superb school, as a start in college."

So what can the thousands look for when a kid named Hoa with brown hair and quick movements gets the ball? "He's fun to watch because he has so much energy and he's so disciplined," said Steve Atchison, the Fergus Falls assistant coach. "We're small. Our biggest guy is 6-foot-3. Hoa is 5-foot-10. We may have the only five-guard offense in the tournament. But Hoa is the point man and he moves the ball, and he's the guy we'll want on whoever is hot for Jefferson on the perimeter. He doesn't score big, but he can hit them from outside, and we tell Hoa we'd like ten or twelve from him in a big game."

Which the game with Jefferson is. The kid from the boat is excited but not upside down.

"The biggest thing about it is that it comes right after we got a letter from my mother in Vietnam. We've been writing regularly. She said she has her exit permit (obtained with the assistance of Senators Edward Kennedy and David Durenberger) and will be able to come to this country, maybe within a year. Each day since I got here I get up and tell myself, 'Isn't it fantastic that you could find yourself in the United States of America?' And it is."

But the gift may be the country's as much as Hoa Larson's.

Taylor jones

"It was hard to believe it was me walking up there in a gown to get the medallion and the diploma. And all the time before that, I was sitting there looking back into the past, seeing how far I had come. I wanted to cry, graduating was so beautiful."
—Taylor Jones, college graduate and onetime jailbird

The printout of Taylor Jones's police record stretches across the prosecutor's office and out the window, if you want to air it out.

It winds from Chicago to Minneapolis and bridges nearly fifteen years of sociopathic jail time. It is laced with drugs, booze, defiance, and blood—most of it Taylor Jones's. He fought with cops, spit on cops, terrorized street bums and welfare workers, stole some, sold dope, sponged on girlfriends, was jailed at least sixty times, got stabbed in the chest, and had his throat slit.

It was not the recommended prep school for college. Taylor Jones was such a hopped-up and violent dude he was persona non grata at detox. The cops had to take him directly to jail because the attendants in the dry-out stations couldn't stand the sight of him. When he went to the Hennepin County public defender's office with his latest alibis, he would carry his switchblade knife. "I'll talk to you," Karen Nasby of the public defender's office would tell him, "but give me the knife first."

He did, he usually went to jail, and he was back in a couple of weeks, ready to face another jury on a disorderly conduct bust. Such a man stood in the North Heights Lutheran Church in Arden Hills this week to receive his bachelor of arts degree during commencement exercises of Metropolitan State University. On the second page of the printed program identifying more than 200 graduates appeared the names of the eight nominated for the Outstanding Student Award. The nominees included one Taylor Jones, once of Magnolia, Mississippi, later of Chicago's South Side, and now a churchgoing citizen of the city of Minneapolis.

"My mother was too sick to come from Mississippi to see," he said. "I'm going back there for a couple of weeks to tell her how it was. She was about all I had in Chicago. When I dropped out of school and started getting screwed up on drugs and the rest of it, there was always a place for me. She said she always loved me but someday she was going to be proud of me. I never thought the day would come."

It didn't come with one dazzling starburst of reformation. It came, to be blunt, because Taylor Jones got tired of losing, being stoned, and running down blind alleys.

"I got tired six years ago. I got tired of being crazy and hating. I got tired of cursing cops and hassling cops and being hassled by cops. I got tired of abusing people and hurting my family and being at war. I was at war with white people and my own people who got in the way or wanted something I had. I hated being frustrated by what I saw the white society doing to blacks. I had terrific resentments because I saw the abuse, especially by cops, and I blamed everybody and everything I could. My lack of education increased my frustration. I couldn't make any progress. I didn't have any chances. I told myself that. I went to Du Sable High School in Chicago. Drugs were the popular thing. Peer stuff. That's what I blamed. I dropped out in my junior year. That's when the dead end came."

Taylor Jones's speech is languorous and drawn-out, nearly hypnotic in its rolling, methodical rhythm, like a low wind in the forest. It is an absorbing mix of street talk and academia. You have to wait on it while he sifts out his reminiscences and his judgments of Taylor Jones, which are sometimes harsh and sometimes funny. His face tells of a weathered, hard-to-define peace. His left eye is almost sightless, the result, he says, of a stick fight when he was a kid. He is stocky and firm-muscled, lightly bearded and totally clear in the head. He majored in human service counseling, and he plans to get a master's degree next year. He wants to spend his useful years saving the lives of black kids.

"It's hard to know where to start when you look at Taylor Jones's life," said Willa Battle of the Grace Temple church. "Here was a guy so far down he had to look up to see the bottom. But here is a man you can believe, because there is no way he could have climbed to where he is without being honest about what he had done to himself and others."

He met Battle not long after he stopped lying and dodging. Taylor was a crafty and imaginative liar. It took some brass to show up at his first church service in north Minneapolis, pretending a sudden, transcending "belief" as his first step toward rehabilitation, and doing it stoned.

"It's what I did," he said. "It happened a couple of times after that, too. Singing and kneeling, stoned. Then I met Brother Albert and Sister Carol Hale at the Outreach Church, and they took me into their home and trusted me. I stayed with them for six months. They said they would be there as my friends. I cursed them a lot for the way they did it. They were patient and kind and looking for the best in me, and it riled me because I kept looking for things and people to hate and be mad at. But all that started to decrease. And that's when I started to listen to the people who turned me around."

One of the people he met for the first time through clear eyes was Taylor Jones.

"There wasn't much I didn't do: marijuana, liquor, Valium, uppers, downers. In Chicago, when I left school, I must have had two dozen dead-end jobs, washing dishes, hauling loads. I usually lost those jobs in a hurry. Doped up. I also took a lot of money on welfare, and I lived off girlfriends. I came to Minneapolis in 1972 because I was looking for a safer place than Chicago, and I did the same things I did in Chicago. I got into fights with policemen and with guys doing the same drugs I was doing. I almost died when I got stabbed in the chest and when my throat was cut. I took every treatment there was, and I kept spending more time under the clock (the City Hall clock tower). I'd get out in the afternoon and I'd be back at night. Maybe I wanted to prove a point to white juries, that I hated them and I wasn't afraid of them. Is that crazy? I almost bled to death when I was stabbed in the throat. Nothing happened to the guy who did it, and I got ninety days in the workhouse for having a twenty-dollar bag of marijuana. That blew my mind.

"I knew I was going to die or spend the rest of my life behind bars. I was down to the bottom line."

Sometime about then he began bringing his rages (when he was drunk) and his questions and petitions (when he was sober) into Mayor Don Fraser's office, and specifically to Mary Lou Williams, then one of Fraser's aides and now chairwoman of the social work department at Augsburg College in Minneapolis.

"Sooner or later every kind of human being came through that door," she said, "but Taylor Jones was unlike anybody I ever met. When he was on chemicals, he was one of the meanest men I ever saw. He was awful. He was so bad he couldn't get in the door of any other department in City Hall. Everybody thought he was dangerous. Well, he was. He once came at me physically. He swore worse than anybody I ever heard. But when he was sober, there was something generous about him. He'd come in with street people and ex-cons who needed help, and he brought in petitions with names of people who were crying for somebody to help them. This guy challenged every idea I had about social relations. He told me once he saw his grandfather lynched. He internalized that. It made him think there was something wrong with him. But I'd listen to his anger. So did Karen Nasby in the public defender's office. She saw something to salvage in this guy. So he talked to us and he began to trust us, one a black woman and the other a banty little white woman, and guys like that almost never trust any woman, period. Maybe it was a start."

When Taylor Jones hit the bottom line, he said, he asked God to help him. He's no preacher. He doesn't quote a lot of biblical verses.

"All I can tell you, it worked for me when nothing else did or could. I accepted Jesus Christ. I mean, I pretended for a while. Then I met people who seemed to see that, and understand that, and they gave me patience. I went to MIBCA, which is a black chemical dependency agency. They saw I was serious and they accepted me. Jim Bradford and Bob Few. Delores Harris of Outreach Church. Kathleen Stewart of the drug prevention at 1800 Chicago. Mary Lou Williams. Karen Nasby. I always liked school in Chicago, but I screwed that up like everything else. People said, 'You can go back to school.' I registered at the Minneapolis Community College. My skills were way low. Seventh grade. But I wanted to stay. I started going to the library. I stayed for hours, reading, reading. Everything I could find. A person named Elizabeth Moore, she worked with me. I said I wanted to learn. Do you know how great it felt to be sitting there with people and learning? It just lifted me. I got my associate in arts in 1987, and I enrolled at Metropolitan, and in two years and one quarter, I was there—I mean partway there."

The graduate.

He means partway there because he wants to study for a master's, he wants to build a life, and he knows he has a message for thousands of kids because he has talked to hundreds already, from the streets to the campus, and they listen carefully.

They listen because Taylor Jones is a hard man to ignore.

———————

Taylor Jones would have earned a doctor's degree. His friends, his colleagues, and his mentors were unanimously convinced of it. But his first priority after his master's degree was the city street, where for months he worked as a consultant and advisor to the troubled in a rehabilitation and mental health center on the south side of Minneapolis. It was the same building where he was hauled in a half dozen times years before, drunk or doped up and defying the world. He survived all that. He became a role model to dozens of young men and women in whose lives he saw a younger Taylor Jones. But he could not survive a massive stroke and heart attack in the summer of 1994, and he died in the place that represented the pit of his drugged rebellions and the restoration of his sanity.

Al jackson

When Princess giggles on his shoulder, the world makes sense again to Al Jackson.

It makes sense even when she cries, which is often now that her mother is gone.

Laughing and wailing are what girls do when they are eighteen months old. That is life and reality. Death and pain are reality, too. Al Jackson knows that. What he couldn't foresee was a moment three weeks ago when life and death would come together in the same stroke of time and frenzy in a hospital room. His wife died, their baby lived. He couldn't foresee three weeks ago that his family would be scattered, his children motherless, each day a plodding search for survival for himself and those dependent on him.

And now it is a daily walk through a cheerless gray world of coping, of telephoning insurance companies and apartment owners.

But in groping through that day, an obscure workman named Al Jackson may be saying something memorable about facing crisis with decency and about the interdependence of our lives.

Each of those days he begins and ends with Princess. And that puts his world into focus once more.

He wakes and hugs and feeds her. At 7:30 he drives her to day care a few miles from his apartment in south Minneapolis and then goes to his job as a warehouseman at a small cleaning products company in north Minneapolis. Each night after work he visits Children's Hospital to see Dawn Marie, a child born nine weeks prematurely as doctors and nurses in St. Mary's Hospital fought to keep her dying mother alive. She weighs less than three pounds, has a hole in her heart, and has Down syndrome.

From the hospital he goes to pick up Princess, takes her home, feeds and plays with her, and puts her to bed. On the weekend he will see the other children, living with relatives temporarily. A few minutes before he goes to sleep, he will think about Dawn Marie's mother and the might-have-beens. And maybe we should think of Al Jackson when bigoted people tell us we won't find many devoted fathers among black guys.

"You have to deal with it," a friend tells him.

He knows that. But what dominates each of his days—in a way that may conceal the fact that Al Jackson is a pretty uncommon guy and this is an uncommon family—is the stark routine of survival. Going to work. Insurance. Is there any way to cover the kids? Read the forms. There is one form thirty-eight pages long. Read the forms again. Accept that you need help. But go to work each day. Al Jackson did that when he was a dishwasher. He does that now that his three-week-old girl lies in a hospital room with a hole in her heart and no chance to lead a normal life.

But she lives. And he knows it was not only the skills and the frenzies of the doctors and nurses that made it possible but the instincts and will of a woman in her final minutes of life. Dawn Marie Jackson, thirty-three, suffered a heart attack early in the morning at a nursing home where she worked as an aide. She worked overnight, he worked days at the Wrightco Labs. Between them they made enough to keep their family of five together.

"The truth is, they worked their tails off," a doctor said. "What happened was rare and couldn't have been expected, a woman of child-bearing age having a heart disease. Her other pregnancies (two during a previous marriage) were normal. She had a heart attack. Tests showed that it was caused by an abnormality of a coronary artery. She seemed to be recovering well in the next few days."

The couple planned to go shopping on Saturday. She was expecting to be released from the hospital that day. She was dressing when she suffered a second heart attack. The hospital's emergency teams came. She was dying. They performed chest compressions, administered drugs, and kept her blood circulating while the caesarean section was performed.

The baby lived. They kept the lifesaving efforts going for the mother, but she was beyond revival.

"The worst part came a few days later," Al Jackson said, "when Susie [their six-year-old] asked who was going to bake her birthday cake."

Nothing much heroic leaps out from the language or the behavior of Al Jackson. He finished high school in Chicago and came to Minnesota because he had family here. He had limited skills and training, but he also had some embedded ideas about the things that deserve respect.

Wrightco is a small company, employing only a handful of people. Jackson does shipping and receiving and handles the warehouse. They don't have Halls of Fame for warehousing. It isn't very dramatic work. "But he's a super guy, and doing it right means something to him," said Harvey Chichester, the company president. "He's careful about every piece of work he does. It's like the care he gives his work is his signature."

Which doesn't make Al Jackson unique. But the nine dollars an hour he makes is a big deal in his life. So when he took time off to go home to drive the kids somewhere in the middle of the day because their mother was tired—time the small company couldn't pay for—it said more about Al Jackson than the resumes could.

"He does those things. He will take a few hours off, too, to help celebrate something with them," Chichester said. "He's really a pretty extraordinary guy. For the last few weeks he's had headaches from his stress. Bad ones. But he wants to work."

A few days ago he brought the four older children together and tried to answer their questions about why their mother had to die.

"I didn't try to give them any good psychological or religious answers," he said. "I don't know any. I tried to tell them what she had
tried to tell them herself about how to live and to be good to one
another. It was the best I could do."

The world of reality runs on insurance. His wife's plan at the nursing home covered the kids. It was a good one, but she's gone. Al Jackson's
plan doesn't cover the kids. In the next few weeks a county social service worker and Chichester and Al Jackson will try to figure out what's
available. There's a possibility of social security benefits from the
mother's tenure at the nursing home. The state has a well-child program that is inexpensive but doesn't cover hospitalization. Jackson might
be able to cover his kids with a plan carried by his company, but it's a
small company, and the resources are limited. He needs to get another
apartment because one of the children can't stand to live in the place
any more. He wants to bring the family back together. He doesn't
know how he will deal with his caring responsibilities when the girl
with Down syndrome comes home, after her surgery for the hole in
her heart.

He knows he needs advice. But he will do tomorrow what he did
today, and somehow his family will come together.

"When I get really blue I can look at Princess," he said.

It doesn't cost a penny. But it is worth the world.

The pranghofers

The man stood barefoot on a stepladder with a meat fork in his mouth and no hands, stringing holiday lights in his yard in Golden Valley.

This was not the neighborhood grandstander in action.

He was a forty-year-old man born without arms and with one leg forced into the hip socket. Skillfully, he threaded each bulb on a wire above his garage door, using the long-handled fork to maneuver the lights and cord. Every ten minutes he descended the ladder, repositioned it with his shortened right foot, and scrambled up again.

Neighbors would have volunteered to help. But long ago they got accustomed to Paul Pranghofer's acrobatic yardwork and self-sufficiency and to the deeds and life of an extraordinary couple in their midst.

While her husband worked outside, Maureen Pranghofer sat unseeing at her kitchen table, dicing onions and tomatoes for dinner. She wore a black blindfold to protect her fragile eye tissue from the glare of an overhead light. With or without the blindfold, the vegetables and the knife she used to cut them were invisible to her. She was legally blind at birth, a condition coupled with a protein deficiency in her connective tissue that has exposed her to one bone fracture after another since childhood.

She has absorbed forty-two such fractures in her thirty-nine years. Most of them she simply left to nature to heal. Disability was her condition of life. It wasn't something to go to war over or to cause her to spend her life mourning. After all, she still had partial, if vague, vision. But several months ago, while getting out of an elevator in

Williamson Hall at the University of Minnesota, she rolled her wheelchair toward the floor when the elevator stopped.

Her limited vision, capable of making out forms but smudgy, failed to warn her: the elevator unaccountably had stopped two feet above the floor.

Her wheelchair pitched forward and overturned. Her head struck the floor, and she lost all of her remaining vision.

These two people are driving downtown with friends tonight to browse the display windows and to absorb the gala stirring of the holiday season. There will be no long interlude of gloom or futility about not being able to join it like "normal" people. En route they may play some gamesmanship, topping each other with horror stories about the current pratfalls of Metro Mobility.

Imagine. Paul Pranghofer is a computer programmer at Courage Center in Golden Valley, working the keyboard almost flawlessly with a punching stick in his mouth, picking up a printout sheet with the toes of his right foot. He drives a car equipped with steering and other controls, such as lights and windshield wipers, that he can manipulate with his toes and feet. His toes are nimble and powerful. Try wielding a hammer, actually pounding nails into wood, using your toes.

This man does it like a carpenter. He eats, plays cards, and opens doors using his toes. His walk is somewhere between a prance and a hop because of his shortened leg. He exudes constant energy and talks in a mellifluous voice that could have come out of Brown Institute. To a visitor, the astonishing part of this is the nonchalance with which he does it all—that and the utter normalcy of the Pranghofer household.

The two of them sit at the kitchen table, rambling on about the day. Here are two people married for fifteen years, dependent on and totally committed to each other in the most profound way, yet each insistent on a kind of mischievous individuality.

She got up and made her way to the refrigerator, feeling in a lower bin. "It's going to be a strange stew if you use what you've got in your hand, hon," he said.

"I want a tomato."

"I know. You've got an apple."

More business at the refrigerator. "No, that's an onion. Lower right. Perfect. On the money. You've got the tomato."

She made her way back to the table and felt the tomato to draw a cutting line. "It was a new one today," she said. "This fellow from Metro Mobility put me down in my wheelchair on Fifth Street. (She is taking courses at Blind Inc. in downtown Minneapolis to learn how to maneuver sightless in traffic). He said, 'I can't take you across the street.' Well, that was beautiful. Here I am in the middle of Fifth Street in downtown Minneapolis in a wheelchair, traffic buzzing around me, and he says he can't take me across. What am I supposed to do? Scare the traffic?"

She felt like Lindbergh. Every day an exploration. She felt a little worse a few minutes later when she collided with an unexpected object on the Nicollet Mall. "Did you know they have plants on the mall? I hooked one accidentally today and brought it down. It was embarrassing."

They met at Courage Center. She was impressed when they sat at the same table and the dark-haired kid, slightly extroverted, collected a prize for their table in a breakfast contest. "He ate twelve boxes of Frosted Krispies at one sitting. It was awesome." Both had been honor students in school, Maureen in Lester Prairie and Paul at Marshall University High in Minneapolis. She received a degree in musical therapy from the College of St. Teresa in Winona and was working on her master's at the university when the elevator accident happened. "Nobody knows what went wrong. There'll probably be some court action," she said. "It interrupted some stuff I was working on, teaching ham radio at the Courage Center. But God knows, there's enough to do."

It wasn't an oath. She meant it literally. The Church of the Open Door in Golden Valley is the centerpiece of their religious and social life. A guitarist and pianist, she writes music for the church and sings in the choir. Four of her pieces have been published, and she hopes some day soon to begin writing about their life together. This is not one of those wistful goals, vacantly expressed. This woman usually achieves what is achievable. She gets to the boundaries. The fracture problem she solves by being careful. "I tripped over a rug last year and broke my leg. They're the kind of fractures I can usually fix by doing my own splints or leaving it to the body to heal. I need to take off some weight. I want to start swimming."

Although she couldn't see it, her husband gave her a glance of admiration. This from a man who was born with defects that deprived him of arms and normal legs. They decided before marriage not to have children after doctors said there was a strong chance of defects at birth. But their days are crammed. He rushes around officiating and supervising adaptive sports for disabled people, and doing his programming. She's going to be attending one school or another. They take walks together in the neighborhood, she in her wheelchair. They bowl together, divide the cooking, and yak all the time. "You hear the forecast?" he asked.

Snow.

"Right. Better get out the snow blower."

How do you do it?

"I can lean into it with my shoulder and flip it around with my leg. It really isn't a problem. You know, the greatest gift Maureen and I ever got?"

Who could guess?

"The gift was each other."

Nothing else came close.

Diane lemke

Anybody can fall down in the snow.

It's not an act that demands great dexterity or subtle muscle control. Drunks do it all the time. So do four-year-old kids. People who fall down in the snow don't usually regard it as a celebration of life. It's a wet seat. What else is there?

Diane Lemke is a skier who gets supercharged falling on her duff. Let the others rhapsodize about their stem christies and schusses. They are artists; the snow is their canvas. Diane Lemke needs no such grandiloquent service from the snow. It's not a performing canvas for her because she can't see it.

Until a week ago the lady hadn't skied at all. A timbered ski trail may be irresistible to a lot of people, but it's an awkward place to travel if you happen to be blind.

She woke up blind one morning five years ago. It wasn't an absolute shock. Her sight had been failing for the last few years of her fourteen years as a diabetic. Her private world, concurrently, was going hastily to hell. She was twenty-five, on the verge of the breakup of her marriage, and now even the pale light and the shadowed images that passed for sight were gone. Her vitality and inquisitiveness, qualities that once engulfed her friends and her problems, suddenly dissolved.

She got depressed, then bored, then physically sick. It was a familiar pattern internists can predict. One of them goaded her back to the workaday realities by needling her for putting on the postures of martyrdom. The doctor also used flattery. When all else failed, the doctor resorted to friendship. She never had to be one of those long-term

139

reclamation projects. The woman's natural temperament is to charge ahead with all flags flying. At the age of twenty-seven she was skating blind, and a year later she was bowling.

She fished and hiked and played golf and the blind version of baseball. She began talking about blindness to anyone who would listen. She did it with the evangelist's pace and zealotry. She had achieved despite the darkness, but she never gave condescending lectures to those who lacked her nerve and exploratory urges.

She hadn't thought much about skiing, though, until the Norwegian Ski for Light ambassadors put her in a pair of cross-country skis, taught her some elemental techniques, and assigned a guide to her. Diane Lemke reacted in character. She was instantly wild about it and the prospect of becoming the world's greatest skier. What did it matter that she couldn't see the trail?

It was enough for this woman to feel the snow when she flopped in it. Falling in it tickled her. It meant she was exerting, achieving. And that was important, not because she could stand up before the grousing normals of the world and say, "See what a sightless thirty-year-old woman can do," but because she has appetites for the open air and cravings that have nothing to do with being blind.

Does she brood now, unable to see the pine forests where she hiked and romped as a girl? "I try to make the memories paint my pictures," she said. "It means something when I gather pine cones now and let my hand run through the water."

She is attractive and talky, a woman of delicate beige hair groomed and cropped carefully. She is headlong and direct, a person who is independent enough to live alone in the house she shared with her former husband but practical enough to hook a ride with anybody available.

It can be reasonably forecast that the lady will storm Norway when she arrives in mid-March as the honored guest from Minnesota in the Ski for Light doings. We intended to chat for fifteen minutes last night at the camping show. Such intentions, when they involve the Diane Lemkes, are doomed. The chat stretched to two hours. She remembered the Minnesota north woods, of course, and all of the sights, from the power of the Lake Superior surf in winter to the grace and fragility of the wildflowers along the trails. She wanted descriptions. How are they now? She asked in a way to make it clear she was inviting no acts of chivalry. She was just curious. The last time she was up north, she said, she felt something she hadn't before, sunfish nibbling out of her hand, taking ginger cookies. She could feel their snouts, and wasn't that great? Wasn't it great for a person to feel a fish feeding from her hand?

Some people, she said, are deprived. They never had the chance to feel that at all.

Chuck lindberg

It was a scene that pierced to the nation's soul, American Marines raising the country's flag in the midst of battle on a mountaintop in the Pacific.

And now only one of the Marines is left.

Chuck Lindberg's life entwined once more with the saga of Iwo Jima a few days ago, and the moment gave him a spasm of loneliness.

The death in Wisconsin of the Marine Corps medic who had led him down the mountain at Iwo Jima, bleeding from a smashed arm, made Chuck Lindberg of Richfield, Minnesota, the last of twelve who shared in one of the most revered scenes in American military history. It was preserved in two portraits, one famous, the other overshadowed.

The first was a sculpturesque photo of six Marines raising the country's flag atop Mount Suribachi on Iwo Jima in 1945. It is graven in the minds of millions of Americans and other millions around the world: the arms of fighting men straining and thrusting the flag upward on its crude staff.

This one unforgettable image declared a unity and a shared fervor among those Marine comrades, bound by the sacrifice of battle and the symbolism of the flag. The scene photographed by the Associated Press's Joe Rosenthal seemed to define the country's own commitment and its vision of victory.

Seeing it in black and white, you could feel the recency of battle, the imminence of more, smell the cordite, sense the nearness of death and the savagery of war.

Chuck Lindberg does not appear in that photograph; he had stood on that mountaintop with five other Marines hours earlier. The flag they raised was the first. Their act was not quite as compelling photogenically. But theirs was not only the first American flag raised on Mount Suribachi but also the first to fly over originally Japanese territory in World War II.

No public squabble ever ensued over which was the first and which wasn't. The Rosenthal photo and the memorial adapted from it were entitled to the honors they received. But with the death of John Bradley of Antigo, Wisconsin, last week, all six of the more celebrated flag raisers are now gone, three of them in battle and three others well after the war.

From Lindberg's original group of flag raisers, three were killed in battle. Two others died well into their senior years.

Chuck Lindberg becomes the last survivor. He is a retired electrician, living with his wife in the home they have occupied for forty-one years. By his own judgment, life has been good and mostly placid through the years of child raising and daily work. During his four war years, though, his life could have filled documentaries. In January 1942 he enlisted in the Marines, a twenty-one-year-old from the North Dakota farm fields near Grand Forks. By May he was in Pearl Harbor and by June on the island of Midway, where a Japanese invasion was threatened. By November 1, 1942, he and 400 Marines were slipping through the Guadalcanal jungle in the Solomon Islands, hundreds of yards behind the Japanese lines.

He was one of Carlson's Raiders, a specially trained detachment of Marine commando and guerrilla fighters, adroit in tactics of infiltration and disruption. It was one of the diciest of Marine missions. The Americans and Japanese were never sure who was stalking whom. For thirty-one days Lindberg and the Raiders fought that kind of war.

His remembrances of it are not theatrical. Lindberg is a droll and self-deflating guy. But he must have been a helluva fighter.

"To this day I don't much admire rice," he said. "We ate it all the time, in practically every version. I've heard all those stories about close-quarter actions in the jungle, all the stuff about hand-to-hand fighting. There was some of that. But I never heard Japanese soldiers yelling in English to the Marines, about Babe Ruth and that stuff. Nobody yelled. If you didn't get them, they got you. I don't like to say it, but it was about killing. It ended up about 400 to 17 in our favor, we found out later. We were supposed to learn some Japanese, to tell them how to surrender. I didn't learn a word. I don't think it would have done any good.

"You know what my weapon was those thirty-one days?"

OK, we surrender.

"It was a shotgun. People don't believe shotguns were used in battle, but they were where we were. We even brought along some bows and arrows. You can believe that. We thought we might need them when we didn't want to give away our positions, being miles from the American lines. I never asked if anybody used them. I didn't. I used the shotgun. I don't know if I hit anybody with it. We didn't usually check that."

By the time the Marines and the Raiders landed on Bougainville, Lindberg was armed with a Browning automatic rifle. By the time he had returned from retraining at Camp Pendleton in California, he was armed with a flamethrower, one of the most demonic of World War II weapons. The Japanese feared and hated it. Its American users weren't exactly enthralled by it themselves. The casualty rate among flamethrowing men was high. Enemy gunners concentrated their fire on them. There was the added hazard of being burned by backflash. Lindberg got scorched once, not critically.

The flamethrower did him no good for the hours he lay on the beach at Iwo Jima in the ninth wave. "Our fleet bombarded them with planes and ships' guns for seventy-two days before the invasion, and they were still dug in when we landed. They had every gun and mortar registered on the beach. It was awful. The explosions never stopped.

But we got away finally, and on February 22 my platoon of the Fifth Marine Division got orders to patrol to the top of Suribachi if we could. It was a 500-foot volcanic cone, the highest point on the island. We got to the top without being fired on. That came later. The battalion commander gave our platoon lieutenant a flag to plant on top. We found a ten-foot length of water pipe and put it up.

"What happened then will stay with me all my life. When the Marines below the mountain saw it, they yelled their lungs out. Thousands of them. It boomed all around the island. It just made you tingle all over. But Marines are notorious souvenir collectors, so the commander ordered the flag taken down to preserve it, and another put up. We had to go down to reload. When we got back to the mountaintop, another flag was up. That's the one that John Bradley and Ira Hayes and the others raised, and Joe Rosenthal photographed. Some people said afterward the picture was so good it might have been staged. It might have been. Even if it was, so what? I never said it was. Those guys don't have to explain anything."

Lindberg was hit by a rifle bullet, which shattered his arm, two days later. Bradley, the corpsman, led him to safety and tended the wound. The arm was eventually rehabilitated. That ended the war for Chuck Lindberg. Bradley, the man he respected above all of his comrades, died at seventy. Lindberg's life may have become uneventful, but it's been one that has never turned its back on Iwo or the Marines. He visits hospitals and nursing homes.

"One thing the Marines left hanging over me. Colonel Carlson put me on report, probation, with two other guys for building a fire under some sake we got hold of. The story was that this stuff would really give you a kick if you got it warm. I'll never be able to tell you if it does. The sake was gone when we got back from the colonel, and I'm still on report, forty-nine years later."

And the echoes of cheering Marines still hang over Iwo Jima.

Baby boy

Fourteen years ago a nameless child was buried in Crystal Lake Cemetery in north Minneapolis under a simple monument inscribed "Jesus Loves You, Baby Boy."

He had been found naked and abandoned near the doorway of a home in a comfortable south Minneapolis neighborhood. The baby had lived for ten hours and was still breathing when his sixteen-year-old mother left him in the yard on a November night.

The child's death and the discovery of his body in that pitiable setting sent an extraordinary grief through much of the Twin Cities and the country. A memorial service was organized at St. Paul-Reformation Church in St. Paul. A burial plot was donated by a seventy-six-year-old woman of north Minneapolis. She said she was moved by an impulse she couldn't explain. The child was unknown and unclaimed. But within a few weeks he created a bond among thousands of unrelated people who in their own way, public or private, celebrated his brief hours of life.

A few days ago, a man of fifty, now living in St. Paul, brushed away the snow covering a small monument in Crystal Lake Cemetery. It was the burial site of his grandson, identified on the monument as "Baby Boy." Beside it he found a spray of flowers and a note reading, "Dear Baby Boy, we still celebrate your short life. Greg and Carol."

It was the grandfather's first visit to a grave he had been trying to find for years. He could have gotten information earlier from news reports of the incident. But in his mind his daughter, the child's mother, was his only source of the details. They didn't meet often. When they did, she was silent about the baby. The memories and emotional drain of her guilt and the pain of the past erected a stone wall.

It's not so hard to understand. There was the child's birth, the abandonment, the police interviews months later, her admission of guilt, the verdict of a public unaware of her identity, and later her two-year treatment and confinement. How do you come to terms with all of it?

A little more than a week ago, the woman, now thirty, relented and told her father where the grave is.

Her father went to the grave and later reflected.

"All these years," he said, "I never really mourned the baby in the way I wanted to and needed to. I think it was the way I found out it was my grandson. The baby had been found outside one of our neighbors'. It was a terrible thing to hear about, but we were simply neighbors who joined the others in being shocked. There was nothing to connect it with us. I remember reading and hearing the accounts of it, but it was as just another reader and listener."

A month or so later the police came to his home. "They said they thought the mother was our sixteen-year-old daughter," he said.

"They questioned her and she admitted it. She said she left the child near a house where a nurse lived, thinking the nurse might find it in time. The baby's father was one of her boyfriends."

For the child's grandfather, and for his wife, the world stopped. The pain tore through them beyond managing or appeasing. When they finally accepted, when they had forgiven and continued to love their daughter, they found that life had changed irreversibly for everyone in the family.

"Our daughter eventually married and now has a family," he said. "She was one of five children. We try to see each other now and then, but there's a strain that we both recognize. She was charged as a juvenile but spent most of the next two years in a combination of treatment and detention, and then she got on with her life."

He works with a foundation in the Twin Cities. Two days after he visited the grave, he wrote a note and shared it with a newspaperman in the hope that it could be made public. It was addressed to Greg and Carol, who were unknown to him.

"Like everyone else in the neighborhood," he wrote. "I was repulsed by the thought of anyone throwing a life away like that. What kind of beasts were they?

"About a month later, two juvenile detectives called on [us] to tell us that it was our daughter that gave birth to that child and left him exposed to the elements to die . . . Nothing was ever the same again.

". . . A lot has happened since then. My wife and I are divorced, our children are all adults, and we have seven grandchildren . . . I visited my grandson Saturday. On his grave I found a bouquet of flowers and a card . . . Thank you, Greg and Carol, for your vigilance this past fourteen years. Be confident in the fact that the baby boy has a family who loves him very much. His name is Michael.

"There is still a lot of sorrow in my family about the loss of Michael, but knowing how the two of you cared enough to acknowledge him in all these years helps."

The child's mother gave him the name of Michael in the months after his birth and death. The Greg and Carol whom the grandfather did not know had stepped forward to stand in for the parents at the burial service, and for each Memorial Day and Christmas Day thereafter.

"Of all the marvelous news the week of Christmas," said Carol Hamlin of St. Paul. "The baby has a name. He has a family to remember him."

Carol Hamlin is a nurse and manager of the surgery recovery room at the University of Minnesota Hospital and Clinic. It was she who organized the service and memorial for the baby.

"There was an obvious need to do that," she said. "But there was also something very important out of my personal life that seemed to form a link with this dead child. One of the loveliest days in our lives each year is to go to this boy's grave at Christmastime. There are the sounds of Christmas nearby. When there's snow, you feel an almost mystical quality there, a blending of time and the yearning to be close to one who is loved. We would like to make that observance with the grandfather this year, and the child's mother if she would like to come. Wouldn't that be a wonderful way to reconcile the past with their lives today?"

A man who had talked to both the grandfather and the Hamlins put them in touch by phone Friday. Fourteen years after his death, a boy who lived for ten hours was still bestowing a kind of grace on people who had never seen him.

faces in the arena

Alan page

Sometime before he became a multi-occupational star, Alan Page must have been asked what he wanted to be when he grew up.

The answer has never been recorded. One possibility: "Everything."

If he ever thought along those lines, he has a reasonably good start on getting there.

It's likely that Page will be elected to the Minnesota Supreme Court. Nobody who played tackle for the Minnesota Vikings has ever considered it. Nobody installed in the Pro Football Hall of Fame has ever had the yen or the votes for it. Nobody who studied law books at night and harassed quarterbacks by day ever ran in a primary for it.

Nobody who is an African American, or a member of any minority race, has ever had a serious opportunity for it.

But opportunity is a slippery word. Page rarely trusts in opportunities. He will be on the supreme court ballot in November, running for judge, because that is what he decided to do, not because somebody opened a door.

This is not to say Alan Page deserves to win in November over his opponent, Kevin Johnson of St. Paul, a county prosecutor who can make a very good case for himself. Johnson thinks Page isn't qualified and that he wouldn't be running without that boost of notoriety he gets from his old jock days. It's a question for the voters to judge.

Yet you can acknowledge that in Page you see a pretty extraordinary man. I didn't say a uniformly likable one or an agreeable one. We're not the hottest of pals. An opportunist? Yes, sometimes. He is cool and he is restless. If he gets elected to the supreme court, there will probably be another goal beyond that. This is Page. He is smart but he is passionate. When somebody asked him to talk to kids, minority kids, any kids, he took them seriously. He went into the classroom with a message: You're probably not going to make a lot of money being great football players. Staying in school, learning, makes the difference in your life. Be serious about it. If you know how to write and talk, you're ahead.

He gave money, time, and energy. He started foundations. He did essays on the jock world for public radio, and they were good. He got appointed to the attorney general's office. And doors began opening. Page opens his own doors. Sometimes he has done it uninvited.

If the doorkeeper on the other side showed no enthusiasm for bringing him into the club, Page usually found another way. He is a systemized man. A systemized man doesn't break furniture. He didn't have to do that to make it onto the University of Minnesota board of regents. Sometimes he got in the door by outsmarting the doorkeeper. Sometimes he outlasted him. In the process, his name rarely leaped to the top of the popularity charts among the custodians of tradition or of established power.

In another time, for example, Page became the best lineman in professional football without igniting a whole lot of personal adoration from the Minnesota customers. He never tried to. When the Minnesota football audiences sank into their annual depressions after a Vikings Super Bowl loss, Page seemed puzzled. The team had played hard and lost, and there were more things to be depressed about than the result of a football game. Somebody a few days ago wrote in to the letters column, complaining that he had been snubbed attempting to shake Alan Page's hand several years ago when Page wasn't running for office. It sounds like something Page would have done: making a statement of privacy.

Being a former football star didn't require him to be a politician. If you were going to judge him, judge him on performance and commitment rather than his zeal as a glad-hander.

But, of course, today he is a politician, which might surprise some of his old colleagues with the Vikings but not others, because he was a kind of football politician. He campaigned for players' rights and mobility. He was aggressive and scathing about it. He was enraged by the owners' arrogance in maintaining a feudal policy of keeping the players in legal bondage. Not many of his colleagues had the nerve or the independence to share his podium. Some of them were uncomfortable with him. He was a troublemaker, rocking boats. So while he might have been a politician then, he was no diplomat.

He was Page, a hugely gifted and driven football player, so good he could change the course of a game himself. He was so good that in the early 1970s he was chosen the most valuable player in pro football—which for a defensive lineman comes as often as Halley's Comet. He was good and he was troubled. They told him how great he was, but paid Francis Tarkenton more. They made him the most valuable, and then denied him the financial rewards. Was that racism? He asked you to draw conclusions. Sometimes he was philosophical and sometimes he was sardonic and sour and scornful. He was Page. When he wanted to run marathons with his wife, he did.

He refused to add the weight that coach Bud Grant wanted, so they traded him to Chicago. Somebody said he couldn't study law and play pro football at the same time. But he did. When he became a lawyer and started opening doors, they said he was exploiting his football visibility.

He may have. He may be doing it now. It wouldn't be unprecedented. He opened another door for himself in Tuesday's Minnesota primary by finishing first in the race for the supreme court seat now occupied by Lawrence Yetka. He ran after winning a lawsuit that knocked down an attempt by Governor Arne Carlson and some of the retiring judge's friends and admirers to extend Yetka's term.

This man who hasn't played pro football for years says he wants to be judged on his career after football, as lawyer, citizen, and man of public affairs and family person. He now will be.

Whatever the verdict, it's not likely to affect Alan Page's self-esteem. Why should it?

———————

Alan Page today sits on the Supreme Court of the state of Minnesota.

Bud grant

Shortly after the 1983 football season, Harry P. (Bud) Grant decided that each man by his own lights should judge when to lay down his shovel for more serious things in life, such as fishing and hunting. He resigned as the Vikings' coach, concluding a career that eventually would carry him to pro football's Hall of Fame. He was lavished with gifts by the grateful Vikings' management, including a deluxe fishing boat. Unfortunately, Grant fished better than the Vikings played without him. Late in 1984, after the Vikings had finished their season with thirteen losses in sixteen games, the management frantically asked him back, offering him a virtual lifetime contract no matter how many more years he coached. When Grant accepted, a feast of public ecstasy followed. Why on earth would Minnesota's normally stoical folk behave that way?

The Minnesota version of orgiastic snake dancing is an outdoor schottische performed on a hockey rink in snowmobile suits.

The Minnesota idea of an entrepreneur is a man named Harry P. Grant, who goes shopping for dog food when he visits New York City and then lands a lifetime contract that may make him the only millionaire who ice-fishes at Gordon, Wisconsin.

Those things amuse migrants who come to Minnesota. They also confound the biographers of Minnesota. But if you understand them, then you understand why the reunion of Harry P. Grant with his public this week produced the closest Minnesota will come to reckless jubilation, which it usually withholds until the ice melt in April.

Minnesota is the kind of place that goes crazy over the return of dull gray normalcy. It was essentially what Grant offered the masses in his second coming at the airport, where he broke the news.

That was all, and everybody shouted hallelujah. Other places demand electricity from their heroes. Grant gives them headphones and wall-crumbling stares. After one year without them, the people were disoriented and lost.

Bud Grant means comfort. He is shag rugs and woolies on a cold night. How many people do you know who will vote against comfort? He means comfort because—as some people were surprised to discover this week—the football team still matters to huge numbers of people. And with Grant coaching, the ball team is orderly and never unsightly, sometimes good, occasionally great, and practically always in the playoffs. He means comfort because under Bud Grant the football team will be a football team and not a squad of Boy Scouts auditioning for Outward Bound survival school.

Somebody asked him a question the other day, this odd messiah in a Marine haircut and swamp stains on his shoes. Does coming back to coach the Vikings rejuvenate you?

Grant dissected that question silently for two or three minutes and then said he never felt unjuvenated. Naturally, everyone went wild from Lake of the Woods to Winona.

All of which bewildered a network radio man who telephoned, wanting to know how Grant could produce such exhilaration in the face of his cold-fish reputation. Moreover, how could Grant justify the professional risk, returning to coach a wobbly football team after nearly three decades of proving that he could coach better than almost anybody?

You can answer the second question in two parts. He was genuinely touched when the president of the team, Max Winter, his patron from thirty years ago, asked him in desperation to do it. So he felt obliged. After which they offered Grant the kind of contract that would have coaxed John D. Rockefeller out of retirement.

His old quarterback, Joe Kapp, had been right. There ain't no red-nosed reindeer flying from chimney to chimney. But there is still Fort Knox. And Grant always admired bullion more than rooftops. The risk of a losing season couldn't have occurred to him. Grant is that rarity in the steam cooker of pro athletics, a man serene with his private lights and therefore unterrified by the thought of losing a football game. Because he is one of those who lives within himself and has come to terms with his limits and his ambitions, he will rarely torture himself over a professional or personal decision. He knows that most of the time he has won or decided right. There's no special reason to believe he won't again.

For a long time his peculiar virtues as a human being weren't as recognizable to the audiences as they were to his players. He looked impenetrable, icy, and unfeeling. The players have always seen him, though, as a person of balance, shrewd enough to know that winning comes faster to players and coaches who are under control. They also know he is as motivated to win as any coach they ever saw. Athletes often live in turmoil, imposed either by the crowds or by themselves. Those who played for Grant came to respect the even rhythms of his coaching style and his personal codes. They trusted him in the decisions he made and the values he seemed to express.

It's why a Grant or a Vince Lombardi or a Tom Landry or a Don Shula would win on Mars if they put a franchise there. Their commitment is steady. So are their nerves and their discipline. Players see that. The security and self-control that coaches like Grant and Lombardi emit impresses ballplayers, partly because most of them are insecure, no matter how great. It's why players we saw as wobbly or unhinged five days ago will suddenly become smart and disciplined, and contenders, next July. You will find veteran football players lobbying again to come here, because Grant provides a very civilized atmosphere in which to play.

What the public has learned about Grant in the past few years, apart from his ability to make them feel good watching quality entertainment, is his instinct for the fitness of things. He demonstrated that in apologizing for being thirty minutes late for the announcement. Being on time has always been part of the liturgy of Grant's religion. Being late this week had something to do with his family. In apologizing, Grant revealed what he thought the world needed to know about his signing and withheld what he thought was nobody else's business, the part about his family. He did what he could to make his superiors, the distraught young coach he's replacing, and even the TV producers feel comfortable.

Among those not likely to be comfortable are Green Bay, Chicago, Tampa Bay, and Detroit.

Fran tarkenton

The line of scrimmage was his keyboard. Like a mature concert virtuoso who understood its nuances and resources, he poured his personality and craft into it for three hours.

He was nimble, smart, and cheeky. Sometimes he was passionate. But the next play he would be the mechanic, adjusting and tinkering. Sometimes he was downright brassy. He'd prefer to call it arrogant, because that's how he sees himself as a quarterback.

To the Dallas Cowboys, Francis Asbury Tarkenton was something else. He was one stride, one idea, and one stroke ahead of them all night. So to the rest of the Tarkenton resume in Dallas Thursday night, you can add maddening and, at the end, unbeatable.

At no time in his eighteen years of pro football has Tarkenton been more empathically and euphorically the leader of his team. The game, in fact, might have summarized the peculiar mix of brains and gall that Tarkenton brings to football. There was his manipulation of the Vikings' hastily engineered ten-formation offense, one that plowed the programmed movement of the Dallas defense into disarray after ten minutes. But before he did that, he put on another hat in the Tarkenton collection. He was a soap peddler. For two days before the game he partnered with the gnarled little offensive coach, Jerry Burns. They were salesmen in the locker room, persuading their football team that these wild spread formations could work against what was last year the best football team in America.

They conspired with guile and joy, and it got to be a contagion.

"I never was part of anything like that in my life," a rookie lineman,

Frank Myers, said after the Vikings' 21-10 victory. "I never thought you could play a big game like that in the pros, people all over the field. The Cowboys are good, but it was like an ambush."

It was the essence of Tarkenton. It wasn't only the football Tarkenton. It was the Tarkenton with his chutzpah and his swashbuckling and his goads to make it work and damn the fences, the drives that were going to make him a millionaire athlete-executive no matter what. With a guy like this, winning and being rich is only part of the grail. Making a joyride out of it is the other.

The preacher's kid from Georgia came into pro football zesty and confident, but also with a likable streak of the Sunday School disciple in him. When he leaves it soon, he will leave still zesty and confident, also functionally hard-boiled, and probably with a few less beatitudes than when he started. He will be heading for the Hall of Fame, and as far as Dallas is concerned, he can't leave soon enough.

The Dallas defense came with its usual computerized sets, ready for the Tarkenton rollouts and for backs coming out at all angles as receivers. They were also going to keep Chuck Foreman under surveillance, and they were wary of Burns's gadgetry.

But what was this?

Foreman and Ricky Young shifted in and out of the I formation. Backs and receivers were spread from Fort Worth to Arlington. On one play they were looking at Ahmad Rashad and Sammy White practically abreast on the right flank. On the next play Rashad was in Arlington and White was in Fort Worth. And the Cowboys were in chaos and ultimately in jail.

And the man who carried the keys was Francis A. Tarkenton. He threw while sprinting and backtracking. He threw on sudden counts and quick rhythms. When they tried to engulf him with blitzers, he threw blindly because his quick read of the Dallas defense told him nobody would be patrolling the field where he threw. And if the ball flew with anything resembling a spiral, Rashad, Young, White, or

Foreman would eventually overtake it. And when Dallas ganged his receivers and invited the run, Tarkenton jammed the run down its throat with Foreman.

For half a season this team had been groping in the crannies and bins for something that would ignite its offense. On Tuesday before the Dallas game, Burns showed his multiple offense schemes to Tarkenton and asked him what he thought. In pro football, the salesmanship starts with a coach. If the offensive coach can't sell the quarterback, especially one who's been there for eighteen years, go back to leather helmets and the flying wedge.

Tarkenton looked at the blueprints. He said at length. "I love it. Nobody programs a team like Tom Landry. We have to disrupt them and make them guess. This does it." Tarkenton lobbied his team relentlessly. Nobody does huckstering in the locker room the way Tarkenton does. He did it one on one, in small groups, in the shower, and across the street over a pitcher of beer.

"It's not gimmicky," he said. "It's sound. The idea is to minimize the damage they do with their safety blitzes and the other blitzes. We have to spread them out and make them move and guess before we throw."

The pros, with all their hoary codes about what works, insist that it isn't formations that win games, it's players.

Sometimes formations help, especially when the players are Tarkenton, Rashad, Foreman, and those all-pro grunts on the offensive line. They help when the Super Bowl champions fumble the opening kickoff and then, with their perplexity mounting, run back another with a runner who lost his shoe. After another fumble, Tarkenton told himself: Hit them now.

He intended to hold off the new formations for three or four minutes to add the surprise element. But with the Vikings twenty-eight yards from the Dallas goal line in the opening minute, why temporize?

Two minutes later he had the first touchdown, and a few minutes after that, another. The Cowboys eventually composed themselves and even threatened in the fourth quarter, but the Vikings defense kept the dispirited Tony Dorsett strung out to the sidelines, refused to let Roger Staubach freelance outside the rushing lanes, and exploited his uncommonly bad throwing. In the meantime they rediscovered major league punting from Greg Coleman and rediscovered something else.

Suddenly, after all the doubts and their backing and filling of the first half of the season, they were together again. It wasn't only the spacey new formations. Those will disappear next week because next week isn't Dallas and by next week everybody in pro football will have spies out for them. It was, if you want the truth, mostly Tarkenton, the nervy, thirty-eight-year-old football tycoon.

They were heading for oblivion with four losses in seven games. They had to be jabbed and butted, and it was Tarkenton who decided he was the guy to kick much butt. There's always a way, Tarkenton told them. Blow out the guy in front of you. Bear down. Make it matter. Alan Page, a remarkable athlete, sometimes smiled at that kind of hothouse talk. But he went along, because if hothouse talk would do it, why not stoke up the heat?

So Tarkenton risked the jeers of the fans to go public in his role as agitator and professional conscience of the team. He wasn't going to be very credible if he fell on his face.

"To hell with popularity," he said. "How many division championships has it won?"

He said afterward: "We can keep winning. We can keep what we have and build on it. We're moving together, Jeff Siemon, Matt Blair, Carl Eller, those guys. A tremendous defense they put together. Who hits better back there than Tommy Hannon and Phil Wise?"

And does anybody today quarterback any better than Francis A. Tarkenton?

"I'm too damned senile to answer that question," Tarkenton said.

He might have smiled.

But he didn't.

Kirby puckett

According to the clubhouse eavesdroppers, Kirby Puckett is talking to his body again. This ranks with the pulsating conversations of the year. Even if it could be understood, it's scary.

Every time Puckett interviews his body he sounds on the verge of doing something reckless, such as getting in streamlined shape to ward off the assaults of old age.

All resources in town should be enlisted to discourage him.

If Puckett had a flat belly, a neck, and a sleek rear end, he would be on waivers in five days.

Puckett has the kind of body that, if copied, would shut down all the aerobic dance clubs in town. If he lived in Germany, he would be in instant demand for TV commercials as sausage peddler of the year. You can profit from this knowledge. Be careful how you raise your son. Give him health foods and he will play for the Catawba Claws. On the other hand, here is Kirby Puckett, adored widely (which is the only way you can adore Kirby) and making $5 million a year.

The Puckster set another Twins hitting record a couple of days ago. Eventually, he will own them all. Each time he does it, they give him a chance to say something electrifying so that it can be chiseled under his future statue in the Hall of Fame to stir the onlookers.

What he does is complain about his advancing case of hardening of the arteries at the age of thirty-three.

He says he is getting old and slow and is hounded by creeping lumbago. There is reason to suspect that he believes this. A luncheon companion of mine brought that up. He said, "This guy chews up every pitcher with the guts to throw the ball. Every time I go to a game he gets three hits, strikes out by two feet the fourth time, throws out a runner at third, and wins the game by himself. He's been doing it for eleven years. He's going to do it another eleven, but he keeps telling us he's old and decrepit. That's a laugh."

No, it's not.

Close watchers of the human species will recognize Puckett's absorption with age and slowing down. It's a nice mix of gamesmanship and hypochondria. Some players pump themselves up by imagining all kinds of physical agonies—backaches, red tonsils, dizzy spells, and lockjaw. It makes dragging themselves out on a field a victory to compare with Admiral Nelson's at Trafalgar. Puckett is a hypochondriac about age. The odd geometry of his body makes it easier for him to get away with it. His body looks like the kind you see in the chow line for seconds at the twenty-year picnics. But when Puckett talks to his body, everybody should listen. The man is a public resource. Without him, Minnesota is Paris without the Seine, Golden Valley without Bassett Creek.

I have a double interest in seeing that Puckett does nothing to smooth out the lumps in his body or to stop stewing about age. First, I spend seventy or eighty hours a year watching the Twins on television. If Puckett didn't play, I'd spend half that time watching the hippos mate on the Discovery Channel. I'm amazed when anybody gets him out. I'm also amazed that he doesn't do more local commercials. The one where he was flying around in a biplane with the flaps of his aviator's helmet sticking out of the cockpit knocked me out. Puckett could advertise Lonnie's Hoof-and-Mouth Remedy and I would probably buy it.

My second interest comes with being approximately double Puckett's age and therefore a little more authoritative about getting older. I never worry much about age. On the Iron Range, you worked for forty-five years, after which you picked blueberries. The only blueberries around here are between the bananas and muskmelon in the produce departments. Because blueberry picking as a reward for hard labor is pretty much gone with all the other lotuslands, I just ignore age. But watching some of the riper characters on my bike ride gives me a closer appreciation of the Puck's wily strategy in grousing about his age.

We've got a guy who's been on this ride for fifteen years. He's got curly white hair and the opaque, hunted eyes of a desert evangelist.

Almost every day he wears a T-shirt with this inscription on the back: "Broken down by age and sex."

It sounds like the wail of the wretched and the abandoned. Everybody twitters when he gets on his bicycle with that shirt. Women, more nurturing, ask if he wants a transfusion. The men look pensive, as though "there, but for the grace of God . . ."

And then we get to some hill.

The man broken down by age and sex waltzes by the rest of them as though they were stapled to the pavement.

This man is no longer thirty-three and he doesn't make $5 million. He couldn't tell you the difference between a beanball and a beanbag. But he's crafty. He knows the Puckster's formula. As long as the Puckster keeps talking about arthritis and the AARP, somebody is going to be crazy enough to go from first to third on a single to right and get thrown out by fifteen feet by the old crock in right.

Ken Covey knows the Puckster's formula. Covey is a retired orthopedic surgeon from Moorhead. He rides in black wingtip shoes and admits being seventy-five years old. This year he showed up in one of those low-slung recumbent bikes in which the rider seems to be doing the backstroke with his legs and skimming the asphalt with his tail.

"It'll give me maybe one or two more years of riding," Covey said, sighing anciently. I heard a complaint from one of the younger people new to the trip. He said it seemed dangerous to let a man so old and vulnerable participate in the ride.

The complainer vanished in the middle of the week in Baudette with two muscle pulls. Covey finished breezing.

Humor the Puckster. Let him talk about the ravages of old age. Ten years from now he will still be bald, paunchy, neckless, hitting .320, closing in on 4,000 hits, earning $10 million, and complaining about his hearing aid. The only thing that can stop him is a diet.

Jack morris

They fought each other to the rim of exhaustion, the Twins and the Braves, Jack Morris and John Smoltz, with the nation transfixed.

And then there was Morris. The old, undefeatable lion. Spears and gunshots could not cut him down. And when the break came, two upheavals hit simultaneously in America. In Minneapolis and the Metrodome, from border to border in Minnesota, the end came in a shock of delirium. It struck with the seismic force of an earthquake. Nobody measured it on the Richter scale. Richter couldn't get a ticket.

In Atlanta, the other phenomenon needed no measuring scale. Silence erupted the moment Minnesota's Dan Gladden crossed the plate with the game's only run in the tenth inning of the seventh game of the 1991 World Series. The silence and depression smothered the city where just four days ago snake dancers and horn-honkers celebrated their Braves' coming coronation. It almost happened. Atlanta made a magnificent bid. It fought obscurity to the National League title. It carried one of the finest American League champions to the limit, and almost beyond the limit.

For Minnesota and the Twins, it was the moon revisited. We're Number One. Again. Worst-to-first. We're historic. Bring on the ticker tape by the boxcar. In the Dome, the walls shook, the air doors almost blew out. People roared and hugged their neighbors, hugged strangers, hugged anybody in sight. They swung their white doilies in a sustained rapture that might have set the North American record for a love-in under a Teflon roof.

And then they piled out of the Metrodome and into the streets, and it went on and on and on into the night.

They had battled exquisitely and relentlessly, Morris and Smoltz. For eight innings, nothing. Nobody scored. The crowd tried to ignite the Twins. But the crowd was spellbound with everybody else. Morris was the aging gladiator, proud, controlled, and fierce; the other, a young man, was composed and unafraid. He had revered Jack Morris years ago in Detroit when John Smoltz's professional career was only a vision. The way it came down, the patriarch outlasted the acolyte. Smoltz left in the eighth. Jack Morris was immovable. He would have pitched into the next century.

Somebody had to win. This was World Series 1991, and it was down to the last game, and there was nowhere for the loser to go except into a numbed trance, mourning the might-have-beens.

So it ended, a World Series that reached unprecedented levels of suspense and sometimes art. For seven games it was carnival and anguish. It was innocence and confrontation. The Braves came in as a kind of national toy and curiosity. They left with the enormous respect of the team that defeated them.

For the fans it was make-believe war, and outside the stadium it presented a serious indictment of what the protesting Indians called the tomahawk tomfoolery. At the end, it was no war, make-believe or otherwise. The fans were drained. The players were drained. But it was baseball, friend. Never forget it. Some moments it was breathtaking baseball, as it was Sunday night in a game that may lodge someday in a special kind of shrine of suspense and craft. It was baseball, both beautiful and excruciating.

And why not? From start to finish, this was World Series baseball made more entertaining and absorbing to the millions by the wizardry of high tech. It was a World Series that gave and took. It gave Minnesota a jubilation day. From the Braves it wrenched a prize that seemed theirs by right, after all of their against-odds deeds.

But somebody had to lose.

If you weren't there in the arena, you missed the percussion and the electricity. You missed the casual goofiness and narrow escapes, as well as the spilled beer. But you took away unforgettable images, sounds, and moments, unavailable to the mobs in the stadium. If you watched in your living room, you saw the faces of triumph and failure in all of their nuances and declaration. The fist-pumping vindication of Kirby Puckett rounding the bases in game six, his adolescent glee; the grinding mortification on the face of Charlie Leibrandt after he failed again.

But the climactic night: It was the twisted cheeks and rock-tough warrior's fury of Jack Morris, trying to get the last gram of velocity on his fastball, the calmer eyes of John Smoltz. The secret huddle in the dugout, Terry Pendleton and Mark Lemke. There were a hundred other pictures to carry into the winter and, for the winner, into the streets.

It was Ball. Prime stuff, with the gold riding on it. But finally there was Morris. A hard man. A hard millionaire. Yet a man capable of publicly talking about loneliness when his marriage broke up. Here also was a man capable of publicly embarrassing his fielders when they made an error, and therefore jeopardized Jack Morris's hard work. Team guy. Selfish guy. Human guy.

He lived the warrior's creed almost as though he had come out of another century. Because of the tempests within him, his sardonic views of the world, he was never going to be the all-American boy.

But was he an athlete? From the scowling forehead to toes. He never predicted he would beat you. He did say he would battle you, and be ready early and late because he wasn't going to let you get away if his fastball still rode hard toward the ribs. And even if it didn't, he would battle. The manager may have given a thought to removing him in the ninth against Atlanta. Morris was tired. He was older than most in this tough man's game. But the manager didn't remove him. And at the finish, he was still there, throwing strikes in the climactic game of his life.

Maybe not as great as some.

But in the biggest game, he was unbeatable.

Despite several skirmishes with the overseas operators, I was unable to break through to the KGB in Moscow this week to promote world peace by keeping John Mariucci out of a Russian jail.

To head off potential riots among his relatives in Eveleth, Minnesota, let me make it clear that Mariucci has not been jailed in Russia. He's still at large somewhere in Leningrad scouting hockey players for the North Stars in a world junior tournament. He is wearing a huge fur cap, carrying a tape recorder, and lobbying the chef in his hotel for breaded cauliflower.

In the KGB manuals, this is suspicious behavior.

Be honest. Where isn't it?

I'm revealing Mariucci's movements today in the hope that the KGB's clipping service in Minneapolis will lift the clouds of bafflement that Mariucci's appearance has created in Russia. Worse, the KGB may have a dossier on Mariucci. It goes back to the days of the Depression in the states, when Mariucci once pretended to be a Communist agitator, ten years old, to squirm into a hockey game.

Nobody in Eveleth gave it a second thought. Any excuses to crash hockey games were allowable on the Range. In those years the Communists were relatively active and planned to turn their protest of a hockey game into a media event. Mariucci milled among the picketing Bolsheviks. Cops arrived. While they and the picketers brawled, Mariucci sneaked in.

But back to the urgencies of world peace. Peace is a frail creature that can be destroyed if somebody in the A-bomb silos miscalculates. So we ought to make sure the Russians get the Mariucci dossiers right.

171

Mariucci is sixty-seven. He is considered the godfather of American hockey because he played it so long ago they used frozen horse apples as pucks where he grew up in northern Minnesota. Some leaders have the kind of face to launch a revolution. Mariucci's face seems to have absorbed one. There's a kind of relaxed devastation to it that reminds astronomers of the face of the moon after a shower of meteorites. If you like pattern stitching, here are four decades of it from flying hockey sticks, pucks, and fists and—in Boston—from dead turkeys from the galleries.

The KGB should be aware that this man is incapable of undercover activity. If you sent him to spy, you would also send Columbo to improve world fashion.

But I got worried when I telephoned Mariucci's wife, Gretchen, and found out about his plans to assault the Russian language.

"He's been taking these Berlitz courses on how to speak and understand Russian," she said. "John has a very high IQ, which he says he showed early in life by refusing to play basketball."

That is marital loyalty, but it's not quite accuracy. Mariucci started playing hockey after a siege of gloom brought on when he was cut from the Eveleth high school basketball team. The word "cut" is used chivalrously. He was the only student who was stopped at the door when the basketball workouts started.

"They wouldn't let me in the gym because I was so rough," he said. "The coach said he was afraid the school's insurance premiums would go up if they put me on the squad."

Gretchen Mariucci sent him off to Russia a few weeks ago with the Berlitz tapes and the fur cap. "It's like one of those Cossack caps," she said. "He thought it would be perfect for traveling in Russia."

The Cossacks were as popular with the Communists, I said, as cavalry posters on the Pine Ridge Reservation.

"I just remembered that," she said. "I also remembered the tape recorder. The more I think about it, the wilder it gets. If somebody in

Moscow has a file on John, they're bound to have this article from an Italian newspaper. It's from the year John coached the U.S. world team in Austria and he got into a fight on the bench with Lou Nanne, who was then one of his players and now is his boss. Looey and John always loved each other. John coached him at Minnesota. But it was rough love, like family. When the team got to Italy after the Austria business, here was this big headline making John sound like some character from the underworld. It said, 'seventy-year-old coach, Italian, Beats Up on His Own Players.'"

Was it distortion? I asked.

"John wasn't close to seventy years old."

Even in Italy, the newspapers can't get it right.

Although he hasn't been heard from since his departure, his wife is not ready yet to call Foggy Bottom in Washington, D.C. For one thing, Mariucci by now may have hypnotized half of Leningrad with his gravelly recitals of life in the ore pits. They may be demanding encores. They may even be cooking breaded cauliflower for him.

"Even if they tap his phone," she said, "there's no way they could get anything incriminating. He's traveling with Bob Ridder of the Harvard-educated Ridders. If one of them calls from the hotel lobby, the phone tappers are going to hear one voice sounding like it came from Cape Cod and the other from the bottom of Mt. Vesuvius. They aren't going to understand a word either says. Besides, John may have so much garlic on his breath they wouldn't come near him."

Which may make Mariucci the last great hope for peace.

———————

The University of Minnesota memorialized John Mariucci by naming a hockey arena in his honor, and his family and friends remembered him in private ways. John died of cancer several years ago. For thousands of Minnesota hockey followers, and for admirers of a good man, John's more permanent memorial is the warm and occasionally wacky stories about John Mariucci—endless and never dull.

x

Norm van brocklin

My telephone rang at 3:30 A.M. in the Sheraton Cadillac Hotel in Detroit on the Sunday of a football game between the Vikings and the Lions. The voice on the phone had the unnatural timbre of a drill sergeant offering a bouquet.

It belonged to the first head coach of the Minnesota Vikings, Norman Van Brocklin, in the first year of his volcanic reign.

"How about some breakfast, you mule head?"

This was Van Brocklin in a rare spasm of congeniality. I said I didn't respond to flattery before sunrise. I added, "It's 3:30 in the morning. Go soak your head. Aren't you the same guy who wanted to fight three hours ago?"

Van Brocklin ignored the indictment and offered no plea. I wasn't sure he remembered. "I got to thinking about playing the Lions with the clowns they gave me," he said. "It wrecked my dinner. I'm starved. I'll see you in ten minutes."

Van Brocklin arrived with the room service delivery man, who was hauling two huge platters of pancakes and sausage. Van Brocklin was hauling a six-pack of beer.

"I'll have a pancake," I said. "Then I want to go back to sleep. If the coach of the football team is going to stay up all night, thank God men of literature have more sense."

Van Brocklin spent the next hour being kittenish and telling hairy stories. Actually, he didn't come to entertain. He came to defend his backside against what he would have called ambush journalism, if he'd been a politician. In short, he was afraid of getting chopped up in the late Sunday editions. Among the surprising blind spots in this celebrated football creature was an ignorance of newspaper deadlines. That was relevant at 3:30 in the morning because the coach had, in fact, threatened to duke it out with the journalist. It started in the hotel lobby. The Dutchman saw the journalist exchanging small talk with the Vikings' general manager, Bert Rose. The Dutchman was planning to lead a putsch against Rose at the time and resented the newspapers talking to the general manager, although it seemed a pretty logical thing to me.

Words ensued boisterously. Van Brocklin invited me to settle it man-to-man in his room. I responded temperately. I told him he was nuts. I said it would get him in trouble with the league and my medical provider. I pointed to the fact that he outreached me by eight inches and outweighed me by forty pounds. He snorted a lot and said I was trying to weasel out. We finally went to his room. I felt like a jockey about to slug it out with Joe Louis. Inside, we wrestled briefly and ineptly, and smashed the TV set. Honor was avenged.

Van Brocklin.

As the night wore on, he got worried. Van Brocklin wanted to know whether I had told the world about our midnight charade. So this bizarre breakfast was really a fishing expedition. I told him I had a better story for Sunday. I said I did a profile on the Detroit coach, George Wilson, an occasional gentleman.

The Dutchman walked out with both platters of pancakes.

Ten hours later, his terribly undermanned team nearly beat the Lions. One mystery about the late Norman Van Brocklin is how so many shrewd television and movie producers managed to overlook a fortune. Television and Hollywood today routinely grind out jock films and series burlesquing the business or recycling some of its myths.

A Van Brocklin series could have profitably run longer than *Oklahoma*. Nobody raged as beautifully and as apoplectically as the Dutchman. He once went into a small town parking lot at 1:30 A.M. to

personally enforce one of his curfew edicts, which was habitually ignored by a wily linebacker. Discovering the escapee's car, he opened
the door to the back seat and pulled the amorous linebacker out of the
outspread arms of his startled partner. The linebacker was docked $500
for violating curfew and $1,000 for being dumb enough to get caught.

The Dutchman's angers were so fierce that a gypsy kicker named
Mike Mercer refused to go back to the bench after blowing a thirty-
yard field goal. He could hear the Dutchman screaming. The established route to the Viking bench from the thirty was on a northeast
heading. Mercer went straight north, through the stadium exit, and
around the brick retaining wall, intending to skulk back to the Viking
bench from the rear. It didn't work. Van Brocklin was waiting for him.
"Mercer," he roared, "you couldn't kick a —— off a ———."

I give you dashes instead of four-letter words not because I'm pu-
ritanical but because Van Brocklin managed expletives that were sex-
ist, bigoted, discriminatory, and slanderous all in three syllables.

When he quarterbacked in pro football, Van Brocklin gave Hall of
Fame performance. He played with intelligence and absolute arrogance.
He knew how to win and he cursed anybody who got in the way,
friend or foe. He brought the same qualities to coaching. Regrettably
it is the kind of job that, to be successfully pursued, demands (a) reasonable skills by the coach's warriors and (b) a controlled mentality
from the coach.

The Dutchman normally revealed neither, although there were
years in which he prodded his scruffy forces to some memorable football. He did that between random acts of attempted pugilism. In training camp one year he swung at a noisy customer who was baiting him
at the bar. The blow missed the customer and hit one of the Vikings'
owners, Bernie Ridder, in the gut. Two years later he swung at a Texas
newspaperman, got distracted during his backswing, and hit a pillar
outside a Birmingham, Alabama, night club. He held a press conference

the next morning to announce that he had been provoked. It was never clear who or what provoked him, the reporter or the pillar.

He brought to coaching one of the most creative offensive minds in pro football, but the quality that dominated him from beginning to end was a kind of supernatural fierceness. It lifted young or mediocre players to levels that were beyond them in their first few years, and made his limited football teams competitive on most Sundays. But the same qualities—the furies, the unbending drive—eventually brought him down in both Minnesota and Atlanta. He alienated his players with ridicule and abuse, eventually became a cartoon in the locker room, and lost them.

But he was much more than a sideline-prowling Captain Bligh. He was a smart and generous guy beyond his tantrums, a man whose biggest failure was an inability to trust. He didn't trust administrators or players and, sadly and finally, he didn't trust most of the friends he made.

His early teams were a mind-stretching collection of football roustabouts and exiles. Leon Clarke, a likable hypochondriac from California, came to the Vikings in the early years with one distinguishing feat in his prior service in the National Football League: He got hit by a falling flagpole in Cleveland. To prove this was no freak of misfortune, in his third month with the Vikings he broke his foot stepping into a gopher hole at Midway Stadium. Bill Lapham, a center acquired from Philadelphia, established his durability early in life by accidentally getting hit in the head with a rifle bullet.

Van Brocklin's teams in their early incarnation resembled less a football squad than a shelter for the homeless. Truck drivers and bartenders tried out for the team. Some of them looked more impressive than the miscellaneous renegades who came to the team from previous NFL custodians more than willing to unleash them. Jim Marshall, who later outlasted all of his peers to become a legitimately great pro football player, almost ended his career in his first season with the Vikings by choking on a grape. A rookie lineman set the team record by quitting after fifteen minutes of the first practice, collapsing in the middle of the agility ropes and pleading with the trainer to take him immediately to the church so that he could make his peace. The trainer bypassed the church and took him to the airport instead. The good-byes were brief.

In the midst of this menagerie, Van Brocklin found some authentic football players, such as Fran Tarkenton, Tommy Mason, Rip Hawkins, Ed Sharockman, Jim Marshall, Mick Tingelhoff, Bill Brown, and, of course, for one unforgettable reprise of his bravura seasons in San Francisco, the King of the Halfbacks, Hugh McElhenny. He also found Palmer Pyle, whose wife, the daughter of the old Chicago underworld figure Tough Tony Accardo, confronted him one night when he showed up three hours late to take her to a team party. Palmer had already warmed up for the party by getting bountifully oiled. He bumbled into their apartment, stretched out naked on the bed, exhausted, and demanded a wedge of the pizza his wife had in the oven. Five minutes later she walked into the bedroom carrying a platter of steaming pizza. She turned it upside down and splattered the cauldron all over Palmer's unready chest and adjacent parts. He howled and screeched. She smiled benignly and expressed regrets that she didn't have any green peppers.

Van Brocklin viewed employees like Palmer with a snarl of resignation and a vow never to be corrupted by the demands of mercy. When he got mad, which was daily, his eyes crackled with red streaks that might have been due to his contempt for mediocrity or to a hangover. It was a coin flip. But although his early teams were usually two touchdowns inferior to their opponents, they occasionally won, always played savagely, and within four years, were competitive with everybody. None of this noticeably placated the Dutchman. He feuded with Tarkenton, muscled the general manager out of the organization, and once accused a defenseless sports writer of unwittingly tipping off the Vikings' first scrimmage play to the Chicago Bears' coach, George Halas. This kind of accusation neatly vented Van Brocklin's chronic paranoia, but it ignored the fact that Halas operated the most notorious spy network in the NFL.

But sometimes the Dutchman coached superbly. When his peers complimented him, he rarely seemed much moved by it, but one day, after his team had beaten Vince Lombardi's Packers, his eyes went damp. Lombardi came into his locker room and said, "It's a tribute to you. You did a helluva job. A magnificent job."

Once in a while he mellowed. He'd walk into the veterans' dorm at training camp and reminisce for hours. His demons were quelled and he was serene, a football man sharing camaraderie with football men. But he quit in Minnesota because he couldn't wait for young stars to become champions, and he later quit in Atlanta because the newer breed sneered at his tirades rather than follow him.

He adopted Asian children into his family. He gave to old football players who were penniless. He was a far better man than his demons allowed him to be when he coached, and although we didn't talk the last ten years of his life because of a trivial argument, I spoke at his funeral with some of his great players and old cronies. I remembered the Monday mornings when we'd ride around and talk football with nothing to grind on and no fencing to do between journalist and coach. We liked each other, and I'll remember that after all the rest.

I don't think, though, that I'd want to make a living kicking field goals for him.

from my family album

Sig olson

In my hometown of Ely, the black steel skeleton of Oliver Mining's "A" shaft minehead hulks somberly above a colony of two-story houses and the frozen surface of Shagawa Lake.

The mining headframe is now a relic, a gaunt museum piece for the passing tourist and for the returning native sorting his memories of faces and muted sounds.

A mile or so from the headframe is the house where Sigurd Olson, the naturalist, lived. Both the mine and Sig's vision and his hymns to the earth belong to the history of this town. Both will live in their legacies. The mine's is in the education of generations that flowed from the immigrants who first worked it. Sig Olson's legacy is the silences of his north woods.

It was a thought worth considering for a returning native who'd witnessed years of squabbling and strife in this town. Some of this whirled around the ideas and environmental evangelism of Sigurd Olson. The mines were the second great battleground. Workers versus management was one collision. The other was more intimate and went to a mining town's heart. Was the mine a dead end for young men or the bedrock for raising a family?

It was, of course, both.

But on this day, there was no evidence of lingering anger. The day was cold but benign. The caverns underground are deserted and quiet. No one has mined in Ely for twenty years. Near the old headframe, snow creates cornices of ironic art on the ridge of a small butte of scrap ore above the tunnels. In them, men in helmets and headlamps and red-stained clothes burrowed into the earth. They did it to feed their families, to scheme a college education for their children, and to share the bittersweet laughter of men working through a dirty job with their fraternal gossip and their fatalism.

I remember their dirty red faces and shaggy humor. I worked with them to help pay for college. I was a kid who benefited from the mine's dwindling treasure. And I worked beside my father, digging the ore out, liberating myself from the baronial power the mine forced on the elders who had families to support and therefore could not dream of college and the city.

There are no runes on the lonely headframe to reveal the shape and quality of the town's passage into a newer time. There is no more rumble of the great caravans of ore cars leaving the mine yards for Lake Superior and the foundries and the worlds beyond. The mine is a monument. Its time, apart from its legacy, is sealed in the abandoned tunnels. Yet the town is still alive with its tourism and shops and workers commuting to other towns or teaching. Its love-hate relationship with the federal government still flourishes. It's a government that's provided the town with much bounty over the decades, but also hounded it by insisting that the wilderness belongs to everybody, after all, not just to resort people and fishing people from Ely.

Yet the frictions seemed softened Tuesday. That might have been an illusion, inspired by the fresh morning snow. Or maybe it was nurtured by the returning native's view of the town from the house where Sig Olson lived on the hill by Wilson Road.

There was never any real reconciliation between Sig Olson and his critics, no meeting on the plains of tranquility. He believed people need and deserve places of primitive nature and calm to bring themselves closer to their beginnings. He believed we can understand ourselves better by recognizing how much we need the earth and its clear streams and its wild calls.

In the town where he lived there were hundreds of people who resented the implication that they didn't grasp those values. It wasn't Olson who made that implication. What they resented at the core was an arrogance they saw, or thought they saw, in people they derided as the nature-lovers. Some of these were the preservationists who led the fight to protect the Boundary Waters Canoe Area from being fragmented by motors and developers. But "working stiffs" had rights, too, the local people said.

They did. The conflict actually was overdrawn. There are huge numbers of lakes outside the Boundary Waters that are open to mechanization. And there's a sizable part of the Boundary Waters itself where you can take a motor today.

And the conservationists might have made it easier with less piety. Sig Olson, though, never saw himself as God's recognized agent in the Boundary Waters battle. He was a botanist, teacher, poet, and paddler. He lived in the town where Slavs made sausage and Finns made their saunas and generations of strong-shouldered men worked like moles in the mines. He ate their sausage and understood their language, and he never retaliated against a critic with a hard or vindictive word. Which may explain why there were so many of them in church Saturday for the services for Sigurd Olson. And why there is nothing harsh or embittered in the house of Sig Olson, where his Elizabeth, the woman who shared his life, is as lovely as always and thankful for their years together.

He died shortly after finishing a snowshoe romp near their home. His last day was a day graced by the woods and by clean, cold air.

A grade-school class examining the lives of great men and women of the twentieth century invited me not long ago to join its deliberations. The price of admission was to come prepared with my own nominations.

I offered ten. The scholars had no trouble recognizing Churchill and Gandhi, but they stumbled over the name of Sigurd Olson.

"Did Sigurd Olson win a war?" a voice close to the philodendron pot asked.

The question was lodged solemnly. These were young jurors probing the qualifications of nominees ranging from Henry Aaron to Ca-
lamity Jane, for all I know. It was serious stuff. No frivolous candida-
cies need be considered. The candidate did not have to be as famous as
FDR, but the candidate did have to affect the lives of large numbers of
people in a special and enduring way. These were the ground rules
suggested by the teacher and endorsed by the class. The only excep-
tion was another kid near the philodendron. He thought the rules
were a little loose and could make J.R. Ewing eligible.

Strictly speaking, I said, Sig Olson had not won a war, if by war
you mean bombs and burning cities. He had not discovered a miracle
drug or caught five touchdown passes in the Super Bowl. But he is
known to thousands of people who feel the same reverence for the
earth. His books are in the libraries and in demand. It's true, they
don't clamor for Sig Olson on the talk shows or put his picture on the
cover of *Time*.

And yet his work and his life have woven themselves into the yearn-
ings of people across the land, most of whom don't know his name.

He was a warrior, yes. His cause was the dwindling preserve of
stream and pine and mystery that we call the wilderness. His tools
were his eloquence and his zeal. Add his Scandinavian stubbornness.
He first saw the danger as a young man more than fifty years ago. The
nation's impetuous progress and its hard-driving recreational urges put
some of its most precious places at risk. They were irreplaceable, and
they could be swallowed or dismembered. His biggest adversary was
the public's indifference. People had to wake up.

The prods he used were civilized. But they were prods. He wrote
and spoke. He lobbied and he testified. He was everywhere a battle
had to be fought, in northern Minnesota, in the mountains of Wyoming, in Alaska. But Minnesota was where he lived. He asked a question. Shouldn't there be someplace, especially today, where people
can go to reorder themselves and to find or rediscover the spiritual

nourishment of the woods and water, where they could see them as men and women saw them hundreds of years ago? There were no engines or freeways or tumult in the street then.

We had made ourselves rich and mighty by extracting from the earth, remolding the earth, putting up smokestacks on the lakeshores, and building palaces in the middle of woods.

He didn't argue with history or the need to grow and develop. If the frontier is there, cross it. If wealth is there, use it.

But save a few strands of it for those who come after, so that decades and centuries from now people will still be able to breathe the aroma of the pines at night. They will be able to see the streamers of moonlight on the water and be engulfed by the silence and magic.

That is still there for us. It's fragile but it's there, and it may still be there hundreds of years into the future. There is a chance for that.

Without Sigurd Olson, there would have been none.

Grandma rose

Her name was Rose. It was crudely penciled with her husband's on a card that dangled from the buttonhole of her coat in the customs line on Ellis Island.

She was an immigrant, a bewildered brown-haired kid from the highlands of Slovenia. The America of her first hours was a whirling, blurred mosaic of alien faces at the inspection gates. Those and urgent, unintelligible sounds that propelled them into their proper lines.

She and thousands like her had been disgorged in packs from the boats from southern Europe in the great second wave of immigration at the turn of the century. They filled the factories and packing houses of an impetuous America. They drilled the tunnels to the treasure house of its iron ore.

They expected to find no gold curbing on the streets, no lemon trees in fantasyland. They had no illusions about where they were going, to the red caverns of the northern Minnesota mines, where a man did not have to speak English to burrow into the earth a thousand feet underground.

I doubt they and the others were aware that in the economics textbooks and cost ledgers of the land barons they bore the label of Cheap Labor.

No one forced them here. If they felt dehumanized by the herding process, in steerage of the ocean steamer or in the boxcars that brought some of them to Minnesota, they didn't rage about it.

I don't know what were Rose's visions in the flower fields of her childhood, what she imagined America to be.

186

Yet in more than four decades of labor in the iron mines, her husband did not speak of life in America as anything abusive or ignoble. His wife became a strong-willed matriarch, a mother of eight who viewed America not with the dewy eyes of the redeemed, but with the unspoken gratitude of one who had suffered its trials to deserve its gifts.

She gave me my first Christmas present and a grandmother's last embrace.

She was buried where she lived for more than sixty years, amid the vermilion earth in the town of Ely. She saw this country—even the harsh daily environment of dark-to-dark mining that ruled her husband's life so long—in terms of the bread and dignity it gave to her family. I don't think it occurred to her that the road ran two ways, that the genius of America flows more profoundly from the conflicts and struggles of its people than from its treasure, and that by this measure, one small but imperishable grain of its greatness was the gift of the lady who spoke broken English and sang the songs of her native village.

Most of the immigrants are dead now or dying, the Balkans, Scandinavians, the Germans, Finns, Welsh, Italians, the others. On the Iron Range, the mines with their twelve-hour days of the 1920s first tyrannized them. But later the mines welded a gruff democracy and camaraderie among the immigrants' children, for whom they became the gates to college education for their own children.

The place had the rowdy gusto of the frontier. It wasn't novel for one or two of the town's ministers to rescue some of their faithful from the snowbanks on Saturday night in order to gather a quorum in the congregation the next morning. But here for three or four decades was the essence of the American destiny—the meshing of the immigrant's hunger for identity with the nation's restless reach for fulfillment.

The mining shafts have been dismantled now. The tunnels have been left to the echoes of the grinding machines and the bantering miners. The old men on the hills have outlasted the pits that might have entombed them.

My grandmother was part sentimentalist, part realist. I'm not sure by what gauge she would measure her life. She lived to see her youngest son win distinction as a research engineer. Before cancer had eroded her in her eighties, she had lived to enjoy the modest luxuries of an electronic age that would have boggled the scared young housewife on Ellis Island. In the fashion of the mining town society, she was the unquestioned empress of her family, standing only a half step below the church. And there were times when even the priest yielded the right of way. There were several tests for an adolescent's entrance into manhood. But I can't remember one that seemed more privileged than when she included my glass in the pouring of wine for a New Year's toast.

The devotion to family up there is fierce and sometimes melodramatic. This does not make it any less real. As it was in the sodhouse of the prairie, the family was the refuge against ordeal, the one unbreakable reality for the immigrant.

There was no gold curbing for the little girl from the highlands. I don't know what she foresaw when she left her village near the Julian Alps. I do know what she meant to us, and her requiem is in the faces of the once-hungry who trusted her and do not want today.

Tyne Souja

In the mining town where I grew up, a candlelight reading of the works of Keats and Shelley was not the kind of event to launch a box office stampede.

Rhyming couplets by the giants of English verse did not dominate life-styles on the edge of the ore pits. But they were lovingly preserved in the world lit. classes of Tyne Souja.

Her classroom bore no outward evidence of being a shrine. It was equipped with the conventional radiator under a bank of windows overlooking the school's boiler plant, which is not the most flattering location for poetic immortals like Keats and his pals to do their daily musings. There was a portrait of Thomas Jefferson on the wall above the teacher's desk, his chest emerging out of the cumulous clouds. In front of Tyne were ranks of lift-top desks, bearing a dozen coats of shellac and the clandestine carvings of scholars long departed.

There was no visible sign of urns or imperishable flames to identify that schoolroom as a shrine. But they were there, and Tyne was their custodian. And I regret today never telephoning or writing her with my gratitude in the years that followed.

I earned very few blue ribbons for luminous scholarship in the lady's literature class. I was not bad in reducing Banquo's speech in *MacBeth* to language that could be absorbed by the teenagers' attention span. But I surrendered miserably when I had to pronounce "April" the way Chaucer wrote it.

What I'm saying is that today I cherish Tyne. Not for the number of lines she was able to imbed in the reluctant mind before it strayed into the clouds supporting Thomas Jefferson's chest. But I do remember the rhapsody in her eyes when she recited. I remember the conspiratorial joy she flashed when she removed one of the nuggets from a line of Coleridge and explained what it meant. And I remember the wonderment she eventually stirred in that reluctant young mind.

She was a stubby woman, effervescent in her readings and rather wild. She had one of those ethnic names, Finnish, that came at you in clumps but sounded much more graceful than it looked—"Tiny Soya." Her hair was impatiently swept back on her head, and when she recited her eyes crackled with evangelism.

Harry Davis reintroduced me to Tyne and, without intending to, exposed my negligence. It wasn't a physical reunion, so I don't know whether Tyne still bursts out in fevers of recognition when she encounters William Wordsworth on Westminster Bridge.

Harry serves on the Minneapolis school board and a million other boards, one of which is the board of trustees of the Teachers' Home on Park Avenue. They have been holding an open house there to celebrate the home's twentieth anniversary and the mortgage burning. Most teachers have no trouble resisting sanctification. In the older days they seemed more remote, maybe because the customs of the time demanded distance between the school teachers and the people who paid their salaries. School teachers materialized at 8 A.M. and disappeared at 4:30, most of the time to do three or four hours correcting papers at home. If they danced or drank or romanced publicly, they risked something awful. It might not have been deportation, although that was always an option.

Society is less rigorous today. Teachers not only fraternize with the people but actually run for office and pound lawn signs and usually can have babies with impunity. On the other hand, their unionization makes them the objects of a fair amount of scorn at contract time. In addition to that, they now find themselves in the era of parental involvement, which often means having to cope with much higher wisdom.

But you can't mingle with a colony of elderly teachers without remembering your own. And for a day or two I have been struggling with my conscience for not having told Tyne about my thankfulness and about Wordsworth's bridge. She introduced us to a magical language and imagery, although we did not identify them in those terms then. For a while Tyne dominated the poetry, with her head flung back and her open invitations to everybody in the classroom to plunge into the same mists of meter with her.

Finally she began to create some pictures for us, which I know was her intent all the time. She connected our adolescent imaginings to the lovely language. And suddenly there was a man standing at the parapet of a bridge in London, the Thames flowing beneath him. And he was speaking.

> Never did sun more beautifully steep
> In his first splendour, valley, rock or hill;
> Ne're saw I, never felt, a calm so deep!
> The river glideth at his own sweet will;
> Dear God! The very houses seem asleep;
> *And all that mighty heart is still.*

What I've wanted to tell Tyne all these years is that each time I'm in London, I stand on a bridge at sunrise, any bridge, until the medieval towers and cathedrals begin to spin slowly around me and evoke William Wordsworth 160 years ago. And I recite each line in a way Tyne might have approved.

Almost approved.

———————

Tyne retired from school teaching after arousing thousands of reluctant scholars to the glories of literature. She married a commercial fisherman in Alaska and, in her eighties, lives in buoyant retirement in Anchorage.

amy

The bride was resourceful. It was a matter of self-defense. With exquisite timing, her escort and father, at the head of the aisle, plunged into a daydreaming trance moments before the processional.

I can make an excuse. My most dramatic recent memories of the bride pictured her on a bicycle seat wearing a helmet, red pants, and grease smears on her nose.

And here she was, luminous and marital, my daughter. I'm not sure what I expected but it wasn't—do you mind?—elegance quite like this. Her gown glistened. Her bridal hairdo, curling tastefully on her forehead, gave her a kind of relaxed glamour and gave me a gulp. Who WAS this woman?

At approximately this moment I began to think about bicycle spokes and sun block.

I don't think it was the ten fathoms of sweet floral fragrance in the church, lightening my head. It was some odd reversion of time. This woman, I told myself, is the same one, who minus a few years, biked with me through the jack-pine outbacks of northern Minnesota, the country roads of Slovenia, and the steppes of Russia. With her sister, Meagan, she was the person who, as my bushwhacking accomplice at nine years of age, stonewalled a porcupine outside our tent in a rainstorm.

So you will appreciate my momentary oblivion there in church with 300 people awaiting the bride's arrival, the groom and his cadres marshaled in front of the altar. I didn't see them. I was still on the Togwotee pass in Wyoming, twelve years before the processional, riding toward the Teton Mountains with Minneapolis more than 1,000 miles behind us. In the little rearview mirror on my handlebar, I searched for movement behind me near the top of one more slope.

In a moment her helmet bobbed around a grove of lodgepole pine, and she pumped laboriously up the pebble asphalt to join me. Sweat bubbles jelled under her eyes and her helmet was askew, so she had to blow some vagrant hair out of her eyes.

"Less than a mile," I said.

The collegian gave it her best Yale-bred estimate of the situation. She peered. She did this partly to appraise the advancing thunderhead, mostly because she was exhausted. She puffed and swallowed and put her foot back into the pedal stirrup. The road had risen 5,000 vertical feet since we left Riverton two days before. We rolled again. The highway dipped insignificantly before the next small brow, and suddenly the small roadside creek was flowing west.

"We're across the divide," I said. "We've gained more than 9,000 vertical feet against the wind."

More bobbing and puffing behind me. Then a voice. "Did we ever seriously consider going west to east?"

Smart kids, the Yalees. The sight of the Tetons was stunning as always, but I almost regretted it, because our journey was winding down. She had been a partner and a companion, and a rather unforgettable one. She had been someone to play road games with and someone to scold, but also someone to rely on without hesitation, and someone to admire. She had been sick part of the time but had not asked for a day off. We tried Bromo Seltzer and Alka Seltzer and maiden aunt's remedies, but she never quite got well. Still, she pedaled and enjoyed and insisted on veto power over the routes we took and the cowboy cafes where we ate. We had come these thousand miles together, and we were both older and younger for it. She had been a pixie and a grunt, laboring up hills for an hour at a time without speaking and then bursting with chatter and plans. She had taken the role of housemother and friend. She had been devil's advocate in preparation for a career in law, and a critic. We had laughed and cried together, nagged each other, and loved each other and learned about each other in ways that were beyond price or imitation.

And the next morning, in the Tetons, we slept well, with no more wheels to turn.

Something buzzed in my ankle bone. It wasn't a bee. It was the toe of the bride's accurately aimed slipper.

"We're going," she said. "Down the aisle. Are you all right?"

Well, sure I was all right. Any father of any bride faces predictable hazards, most of them well documented and first witnessed by the cavemen. The cavemen actually had a breeze. The social order was more structured, the trappings of the wedding more compact. One danger from which the cavemen seemed reasonably insulated was the creative bride. The danger, of course, is rampant today. It can be compounded into infinity when the creative bride happens to be a lawyer.

Calling this bride dangerous does not meet the test of fairness, I'll concede today. What she was, with the full complicity of the groom, was relentless. Her wedding was going to be a blend of the traditional and the mildly wacky. It was going to be fiercely inclusive and nonsexist. The father of the bride would not hog all the honors in the processional. He and she would be accompanied by the mother of the bride. The flower girl was not going to be the flower girl. "That's a role," the bride said. "It's cute. But it puts little girls in a box."

The father of the bride listened to this wisdom without argument. What was I supposed to do, get an injunction?

I settled for "what will you call her?"

"She should be called the bearer of flowers, rings, and all good things."

Will she?

"Certainly. There are a few other things. You have this business of calling the groomsmen 'best men,' while the bride's attendants are called 'bridesmaids' or something just as medieval. That's lost its place in today's wedding."

You're throwing out the best men?

"Not at all. John and I are keeping the best men. We're just changing the description of the female support group. Our combined male and female witnesses will be called the best men and better women."

Amy Klobuchar and John Bessler, also a lawyer, appeared unexpectedly in the pew behind me at a church service in spring. I congratulated both on having discovered humility in confessing their sins. They said, yes, that was nice, but they were actually casing the church as a site for their wedding. I made the obligatory show of amazement and thanksgiving, which was sincerely felt. John Bessler is an engaging, bright, and thoughtful young man. My daughter, although a careerist, has the conventional biases in favor of marriage.

The engagement took place, they explained, in the nonfiction section of the Hungry Mind bookstore in St. Paul. So here was my first daughter, the princess of marshmallows in her days with Campfire Girls, about to launch herself into the trackless wilderness of matrimony. She said the father of the bride certainly had prerogatives. One of these was the right to share in the expense of the wedding. Never have I been made to feel so honored in the presence of a touch. She assured me that prudence would reign, and I suppose it did. The guest list was limited to between 300 and 400. The Hubert Humphrey Institute was chosen for the reception.

A few months before the event, I got a telephone call from my daughter. "I just read the papers. Do you know what's happening the week of our wedding? There's going to be a convention in Minneapolis. We've got to book hotel rooms for eighty out-of-town guests the same week when 30,000 Lions are in town. It's a disaster."

It fell short of that. The couple got all the rooms that were needed, and they forged on. The church was University Lutheran Church of Hope in Minneapolis, large and warmly renovated. The wedding program was enhanced by an insert containing brief profiles of the attendants. It was saucy and full of the adolescent gossip of old friends. It was a remarkable document. Among other things, it introduced the guests to Amy Scherber, one of the better women, now a world-ranking bread chef. It might have been the first wedding program in history that contained a commercial for a Manhattan bakery.

To spare the out-of-town guests from wilting in boredom in the hours before the twilight ceremony, the bride and groom engineered a morning canoe safari for the more nautical guests and a stroll in the University of Minnesota arboretum for the swamp foxes. Parents of the bride and groom were deputized to lead the explorers. But by 5 P.M. we were all sequestered in the church, and the sun poured benevolently through the stained glass. The bride was glorious, the groom was courtly, and Mozart, Bach, and the bearer of flowers, rings, and good things sparkled. The pastor, Mark Hanson, complied with the bride's writ of mandamus and made no jest about the one hundred lawyers swarming the seats, which says much about the disciplines of the cloth.

Five steps down the aisle, I felt another, sharper pain in my ankle. Migawd, I told myself, it is shin splints. What a time!

It wasn't shin splints. It was the bride's pointed slipper again, delivering a clandestine kick in the leg. "You're going too fast," she said. "I don't take this walk every day. This isn't a two-minute drill, for Pete's sake."

I want you to know that before the wedding I got out of the Horatio Hornblower outfit I wore for the canoe safari. I showed up at the church in a blue-gray business suit with a stylish tie.

You should have no doubt about who picked out the tie.

Father mike

His neck always looked too large for the clerical white collar he wore. It was a squeeze that might have given Frank Mihelcic's face its chronic tone of sunburn red.

He was the Catholic priest in my hometown for more than fifty years. His language was more sanitary than General George S. Patton's, but their styles were roughly the same. Patton charged head-on through enemy armies, guns blazing. Father Mike handled sin and backsliders about the same way. Neither took many prisoners.

The roster of Catholic priests who have received the Hollywood treatment is big enough to cause congestion both in heaven and at the box office. We've seen fist-swinging waterfront priests, crooning priests, living saints, and frocked avengers charging outs of trenches carrying rosaries and machine guns. Later, the movies discovered crooked and abusive priests, but nobody pretended that all of these versions were typical, and one thing is certain:

Hollywood never summoned the nerve to ask Frank Mihelcic's permission to portray him. And because it didn't, none of the penitents whose souls he tried so robustly to save could ever look seriously at the mining town priests invented by Hollywood.

In Ely, Father Mike represented God, discipline, social justice, and the therapeutic power of the collection basket as a means of granting peace of mind and rewards thereafter.

In full flight of a sermon on the commandments or on his parishioners' excessive thrift at collection time, Father Frank Mihelcic reached levels of inspired wrath seldom attained by the prophets. Politicians quailed before his assaults on hypocrisy in city hall. Politically Correct Thinking reigned in those years under different labels, and it was supposed to be wrong and unconstitutional to mix politics with salvation. Frank Mihelcic ignored those injunctions without breaking stride.

Did judges on their benches know more about crooks than Father Frank Mihelcic in his confessional box?

Yet while he never denied being dictatorial as God's hardiest agent in Ely, Frank was never imperial. He was tough and smart, but first he was devout. He commanded a unique power and control in an essentially frontier town of volatile politics and ethnic goulashes, but he was first a servant.

He'd rail from the pulpit at such mixed targets as the hemlines of the flashier parishioners at High Mass and the all-night Saturday pinochle parties that left some of the flock in no condition for church the next morning. He demanded high attendance in the confession lines on Saturday afternoon and more enthusiasm in the hymnal sing-alongs. When Frank ran his church, there wasn't much talk about the social struggles that dominate church sermons today: marital strife, sexual preference, women's rights, abortion—none of that had reached the national conscience during Father Mike's stewardship. But confronted with his people in trouble, those who were battered emotionally or financially, he was soft as pumpkin.

He pulled more than one drunk out of a snowbank on a Saturday night, posted bail at the courthouse, and went into his own pocket when a widow couldn't make a payment.

The psychologists later created a category for the relationship that Father Frank Mihelcic had with his congregation for fifty years, through six masses every Sunday, one of them in the Slovenian language. The psychologists called it tough love. He'd have accepted that idea because when he was a young priest not far removed from his native Slovenia, the mining towns of northern Minnesota virtually demanded it.

It wasn't that sin was any more popular then, although the liquor licenses certainly were. The environment was hard-barked. The hours in the mines were long. The work was dangerous, and until the mid-1950s, the pay was grudging. The neighborhoods rang with dialects and cultures. If the priest or minister in town was going to be believable, he couldn't afford timidity. He couldn't afford it, especially, if he was ever going to build the new church that would be a sort of consecration of his life work. Nobody accused Father Mike of timidity. He baptized, confirmed, and buried. For thousands of people spread out over three generations, he was more the heartbeat of the town than the mines that gave it a payroll and the woods and water that gave it gentleness.

In a way, he reflected both, the implacable hard earth but also the more enduring nourishment of the nature around it. He gave me my baptism, first Communion, and confirmation. Apart from my parents, his was the most memorable face from my childhood and adolescence and the most influential. I later moved under another roof to worship. But I never tried to separate myself sentimentally from those beginnings.

The child found out early that there was nothing much to be afraid of from Frank Mihelcic as long as you went to Mass, took Communion, respected your parents, and, when the time came, made a reasonable showing at collection time.

When you look at his mission today, the social doctrines and strictures it tried to impose were medieval. So he might have been both strength to his people and a defender of ignorance. Those are questions for another venue. But he finally got his beautiful church for which he'd worked forty years. A squadron of priests from coast to coast attended the dedication service. They were joined by hundreds of people who had listened to his booming petitions in two languages on Sunday morning. They were the ones who had also received his comfort when only the understanding in Frank Mihelcic's big, beefy face could make a grief bearable.

The clerical scholars tell us the times today can't support a Father Mike of his style and force. I'm not sure of that. The Father Mikes sometimes create the times.

The potica-makers

About now on Christmas Day they would be passing the platter of strudel in the mining towns of the north.

Nobody in Ely, Minnesota, called it strudel, which is a delicate and tasty German pastry. That name reminded too many of the mining families of the Austrian occupation of Slovenia in the former Yugoslavia a century ago. So they had their own word for it. Slovenia is where hundreds of them were born. They were brought to America on big ocean liners and unloaded at Ellis Island for the beginning of the great adventure in the land of bounty.

The land of bounty didn't give them jewels and nectar, but it did give them iron. They didn't find it on sidewalks. It was 1,500 feet below ground, and they spent the rest of their working lives as helmeted cavemen carrying picks and sticks of dynamite. They felt their way underground with ghostly carbide lamps wrapped around their foreheads, probing the dust hanging in the damp air after the dynamite brought down fifty tons of the tunnel wall.

It was dangerous work in the early years, but it fed their families, and some days they partied. Christmas was one of them.

The dancing, of course, was for other days. On Christmas, the missus brought out the potica, which in its purest form is dark nutbread, usually made with crushed walnuts and typically eaten with fresh-baked ham slices. Let me spare you a hopeless wrestle with those alien syllables. The word is pronounced po-TEE-tzah, and roughly rhymes with Lolita. In its hybrid version it was the Austrian apfel strudel, a dessert roll made with dough rolled so thin it was possible to hold it up to a kerosene lamp and read the lampmakers' factory address through it. It was layered with cheese, nuts, and apple paste, rolled into spirals, coiled into a pan, and baked amber and crisp.

I'm telling you this not to strum the harp chords of the long ago Christmas but to ease the sweet agonies of the woman who called a few days ago, wondering whether anybody still makes this stuff and how could they deal with Christmas without it on the Iron Range.

The answers consecutively are yes and moot. They don't have to face a wasteland of Christmas without potica because somebody made it this year. I don't think it was my mother. She is eighty-six and has lost some of her agility with the rolling pin. She was once one of the local Michelangelos of potica making. Doing it right required more than tireless wrists. It needed creativity and management skills and mathematical precision of the kind the great Florentine needed to paint the Sistine ceiling.

This was so because by the time the dough was fully rolled it had a circumference wide enough to hold a square dance. Most families owned a dining table that was adequate at least for the first stages of the rollout. After that, a rough rule of aerodynamics took over. How far did the tabletop lie above the floor, and could the dough handle the tension of hanging in sheets, surrounding the table. It fell in great cascades of translucent drapery, inching toward the carpet.

The beautiful part of the suspended potica dough was its versatility. It was not only the first phase of a strudel. Its folds also gave unbeatable concealment when we played hide-and-seek.

Every family in the neighborhood laid in arsenals of potica for Christmas. By midafternoon the annual carousel of house calls was underway. The adults moved from neighbor to neighbor, crunching through the snow and wishing Merry Christmases and bringing samples of strudel or potica. The calorie consumption must have shot past the red zone and off the board by twilight.

With the strudel, most of them lugged gift jugs or Mason jars filled with the family wine. There were vats and barrels in practically every basement. Some of the more energetic vintners made their wine out of the pin cherries growing wild and available free to pluckers who explored the woods between town and the lake country that eventually became the Boundary Waters Canoe Area. Most of them bought crates of Michigan grapes trucked into town by the Casagrande company in Virginia.

Nobody really bothered to read the law on the production of homemade wine, including the local wardens of justice. It was assumed that once the flowage reached a certain level, it was technically illegal. So everybody discreetly advised the Casagrandes to deliver after dark. This was an aimless precaution because, by the time one of those six-wheeled beasts made the turn past Lampert's Lumber Yard and chugged into an alley by moonlight, everybody in town knew where it was unloading and how much, including the local wardens of justice.

The wardens rarely displayed much alarm about who was getting what. One reason was that the wardens themselves usually put in an order to the Casagrandes sometime in June and took delivery about the same time everybody else did.

You might have had to be Slovenian to make the strudel and potica, but you didn't have to be one to eat it. The other ethnic clans were sharing their own concoctions in the other mining locations in town, and when the stars were out full blaze the nationalities began crossing the imaginary boundaries. So it was that before Christmas night was out, it had become a merging and sharing of the foods and cultures. Somebody would bring out an accordion, and the holiday folk ballads of northern and southern Europe sounded with the mingled voices of the new America.

That may have been a more profound bounty than jewels and nectar.

minnesota touches the world

Dave simonson

Of all the ominous sounds in nature, nothing grips the attention of the bush traveler as emphatically as the booming of a hungry lion.

There is something about the total conviction of that sound. It is nearby and awesome. It puts bubbles in your skin and little whirlpools of electric tension in your glands and guts.

The lion was a few hundred feet away. It was conscious of our footfalls and scent as we passed through the thorn bushes by starlight and flashlight just before daybreak in the East African bush country. When a lion is that close, you are not inspired to do a psychological analysis of the beast's intentions. I couldn't avoid the thought, though, that this one was lonely. The clue was the answering call from a second lion a few hundred feet on the other side of our track.

So the lions pretty well had us straddled, and we could only guess at the significance of the grunts and bellows they were exchanging across the tall grass of the Engaruku Basin in Tanzania. The Reverend Dave Simonson, hauling a Ruger Blackhawk .357 in his holster, decided that instead of being spread out on the trail as we were, we should present a moving huddle of flashlights to the growling inhabitants.

"Are they ready to feed?" I asked.

"Probably," he said. "I don't think they've eaten overnight. We shouldn't have much to worry about if we stay together like this and let them know we're here."

It was not what you would call a sweeping guarantee. But when the reverend speaks he does it in one of those deep, authoritative baritones that arouses as much faith as hope. So we walked through the valley of the roaring lions and into the sunrise.

I will tell you this about the roar of a lion when it is close, and all that stands between the two of you is a few yards of blowing grass and a fourteen-dollar flashlight from Target: I have heard approaching freight trains when my car neared a crossing. I have heard ten-ton falling boulders on a mountain wall overhead, and I have heard lightning bolts splitting trees in the backyard. I will take the freight train, boulders, and lightning bolt miles ahead of the roaring lion in the African bush.

It is a sound that cuts through your bones and spins your stomach. Even hundreds of yards away it is amplified with a kind of wraparound thunder that you might experience if they put the lion in the middle of the Omnitheater in St. Paul. When it's truly close, it seems to shake the ground under you.

But by the sunrise, the ground had by and large rearranged itself. The lions had gone and the reverend led a two-minute devotion. He never was dazzled by long sermons.

You don't want to get the idea that we have been walking through the gazelle herds and mud huts like a bunch of apostles. The reverend knows the language of the barnyard as well as the pulpit.

You're not going to find many copies of David Simonson. I'm not sure Christendom is ready for it, at least the Lutheran branch of it. He is beefy, gregarious, and devout. He is savvy in the laws of the jungle and absolutely unbending about his lifelong commitment to bring something better into the lives of these people, and he is instantly recognized by scores of Africans we meet, the ones carrying hymnals as well as bows and arrows.

He is also a passable autocrat and showman. He was taking us through the East Africa of summer 1988. Except for the six trekkers threading through the acacia forest on their way into the rift, was it any different than it was a thousand years ago?

Yes and no. The wilderness was almost the same. Those sounds in the night, the screams of one animal yielding to the superior strength and urgency of another, were about the same.

But the reverend, among other things, made it different. Dave Simonson wore a white beard and an Australian outback hat that conveyed a mixed image of John Wayne, Ernest Hemingway, and Crocodile Dundee. He had vast shoulders and a bountiful gut and he waddled a little when he walked. He walked with remarkable velocity for an overweight fifty-seven-year-old preacher, and with uncommon good humor for a man leading us into a land of poisoned-arrow hunters.

"The Sonjo people," he said. "The little guys with the poison arrows. They're friends of ours. So are the Masai. But the Masai are plains people. They don't go into the hills after the Sonjo cattle because they can't drive them over the escarpment without risking those poison arrows."

So we had nothing to worry about from poison arrows. These were people, after all, now conditioned to Westerners—missionaries, traders, explorers, hunters, and finally tourists. The Sonjo don't find many tourists rubbernecking in the African Rift. The rift is that 4,000-mile-long fissure in the earth's surface, nearly thirty miles wide, running from the Red Sea to the edge of the central African jungle. It was created by a vast volcanic power whose aftershocks are still evident in random eruptions of volcanoes we will pass in our 200-mile walk from Loliondo to Arusha.

We are doing it not because we're strange for lava dust or intrigued by poison arrows, although some of the baffled villagers en route confessed that suspicion, but because the reverend is a special kind of dreamer.

He is the kind of dreamer with the red clay of Tanzania under his nails and sweat in his armpits and a steady hand on the Ruger .357, but a dreamer still. He sees clinics and classrooms in the villages of the Masai and Sonjos and the others. He sees babies with something more in life than malaria and lung disease. The reverend does more than see the hospital and schoolroom. He builds them. Specifically he collects money and technology and he nourishes the trust of the villagers.

207

Together these have produced hundreds of schoolrooms and a handful of clinics that have brought health and perhaps the greater miracle of learning to thousands in the past twenty years. We were there to raise money for those schools and hospital rooms by obtaining thousands of dollars in pledges from people back home.

Our small clan was notably free of saints. Dick Hefte is a fifty-seven-year-old lawyer from Fergus Falls, Minnesota, and a friend of Simonson's. Kjell Bergh is an auto dealer and travel service operator from Edina, associated with the Simonson family in the operation of a safari lodge in Tanzania, and also the husband of a Tanzania-born artist and folk dancer. Donna Reed is a former librarian and socialite in Atlanta, now committed to African causes. Mark Jacobsen is a medical doctor, born in Stillwater, and now director of Masai Medical Services in Arusha, Tanzania. I can be classified as even less saintly than the others. But I have seen enough of bootstraps schoolrooms and clinics to know that walking 200 miles in the rift to dramatize the need for more is worth the wobbly knees.

"What were you saying about the route today, Reverend?"

"Today we have to worry only about snakes, leopards, and tsetse flies."

It sounded like a promising disaster.

"I've got the Ruger because you never know when you're going to surprise something and make him inhospitable," the reverend said. "I'm talking lions and leopards."

It's been more than thirty years since his first encounter with a lion. Simonson came out of Concordia College in Moorhead, Minnesota, and the Lutheran seminary to feed mouths and save souls in that specific order. His wife, Eunice, came with him to tend sick babies and mend broken bones. They were still charged with idealism when the elders of a Masai village to which they wanted to bring the wisdom of Martin Luther asked him first about his shotgun.

A lion had attacked the village twice, causing injury. He would come a third time to kill, they were positive. They even told the missionary novice where the lion would come and when. They asked if he could help. They were serious, and the reverend was scared, but he said he would. At dusk he parked his Land Rover outside the village. Shortly before sunset he heard the lion coming. Grunting and sniffing, it stopped and crouched. Simonson dismounted. He had never fired the gun, had never seen a lion that close in the wilderness. When the lion was thirty feet away he fired. The big black-maned cat fell dead. The young missionary was still trembling when the Masai villagers arrived with their shouts and tears of thanksgiving.

Not all of those Masai villagers are Christian converts today. But some are, and you're never going to convince them that there isn't something close to miraculous about Dave Simonson.

He disavows any of that, of course. But in thirty years he has become famous both in mission circles and among thousands of African villagers to whom he and his wife and their colleagues have brought health, schoolbooks, and the message of God.

With Simonson, we'd walked and walked and filled our heads with sensations to last the rest of our lives. And now the last palisades separating us from our destination in Arusha lifted before us.

It had been demanding. It had also been hilarious here and there. By night our blisters needed the kind of care you would expect in a tire shop. We spent a fair amount of convalescence time each day repuncturing and patching and reapplying swabs of tenderness, the result of the daily twenty-to-twenty-five-mile hauls. We consumed gallons of fluid en route daily, so that the most popular man on the trek was the little Tanzanian who filled our canteens from a barrel at each stop, using a suction and siphon system with an orange rubber hose. It didn't look all that sanitary, but nobody was going to argue.

We offered a prayer at the beginning of each day, compliments of the reverend or whoever was the designated petitioner. It was always a comfort and always a reaffirmation, because each small ache and groan seemed to caricature the difference between the superficial hardship we felt and the life of burden we saw in each village where we walked. And yet we were welcomed invariably with a smile and a courtesy. And the geniality deepened when the villagers discovered that the heavy-footed minister and the "daktari," Dr. Mark Jacobsen, both spoke their language and understood their friendship.

In the final twenty-four hours, Africa gave us a mural of its stunning geography, its pain, history, yearning, and hypnotic force. Near a Masai village we were greeted by a warrior who had attended a Christian primary school and then returned to his tribe. He felt comfortable with us, and we talked about Africa and America. He had recently killed a lion. The warriors had formed a circle. As it prepared to lunge, he planted the end of his spear in the ground and the lion sprang, impaling itself on his blade.

"Were you afraid?"

The Masai smiled in genuine mystification. "You cannot have fear facing the lion," he said through Mark Jacobsen. "Killing the lion is customary."

We entered moody scrubland as we came out of the rift. The perpetual wind created spiraling dust devils rising hundreds of feet in the air. And then walls of silt turned day into dirty brown. We lunched in the dust-filled classroom of a stone schoolhouse the Canadians built four years ago. A pupil's notebook was lying on a bare bench that served as a desk. In carefully crafted letters the young Masai boy had made notes about how to write a letter in English. And now this same boy was somewhere on the great plain, standing watch over a herd of cattle as his ancestors had done for hundreds of years.

"We don't want to change their cultures," Dave Simonson had said. "We just want to find a way to give them the physical things—the schoolrooms, books, blackboards—that will make it possible for them to learn things that will give them a better chance for health and safety and a broader life, if that's what they'd like. I don't know how we can presume to say that we know more about living a wholesome life. They have three main relationships in their lives, their human relationships, the one with their environment, and the one with God. They're serious about all of them. Sometimes we aren't."

With a Masai schoolteacher acting as guide, we scaled an 800-foot escarpment that vaulted us out of the great rift and onto a vast meadow where herds of goats and cattle grazed. Mountains rose in all directions. It was the kind of scene you might experience in central Montana, except that here there was the inferno of the desert gorge just behind us, the everlasting snows of Kilimanjaro to the east, thatched villages just above us, and giraffes, gazelles, ostrich, hyenas—and roaring lions—not many miles away. It was hard for the brain to hold all of that in one week.

But when we arrived on the outskirts of Arusha, 200 miles and eight days from where we started, we walked beneath groves of bougainvillea and flame trees. The reverend had been trying to explain it. If you dream enough, the beauty in Africa outlasts the pain.

In one of his rare few minutes of leisure in 1992, Dave Simonson considered the allures of retirement from his African missionary work. It would mean hunting and fishing forays from the family home in Fergus Falls, Minnesota, some part-time pastoral work, and reacclimation to the thrills of driving freeways. He survived these dangerous thoughts with the not-so-gentle intervention of his Masai friends and the distant sound of lions at daybreak. He and Eunice did reduce their work schedules somewhat to allow time for two annual visits to the states—partly to work on the house in Fergus Falls, but mostly to raise money for the kids and the sick in Africa. The reverend underwent bypass surgery in the Twin Cities in 1994 and returned to Tanzania with Eunice three weeks later.

Pfeifer-Hamilton Publishers produces quality gift books celebrating the special beauty and unique life-style of the north country.

Bob Cary
Tales from Jackpine Bob
Root Beer Lady

Shawn Perich
Fly-Fishing the North Country
Fishing Lake Superior
The North Shore

John Bates
Trailside Botany

Kate Crowley and Mike Link
Romancing Minnesota

Scott Anderson
Distant Fires

Nadine and Craig Blacklock
The Duluth Portfolio
Gooseberry

Sam Cook
Up North
Quiet Magic
CampSights

Laura Erickson
For the Birds

Mark Stensaas
Canoe Country Wildlife

Call us toll free at 800-247-6789 for a complete catalog.

Pfeifer-Hamilton Publishers
210 West Michigan Duluth MN 55802-1908